FEEL GOOD NAKED

FAIR WINDS
PRESS
GLOUCESTER, MASSACHUSETTS

FEEL GOOD NAKED

10 NO-DIET SECRETS TO A FABULOUS BODY

Laure Redmond

FAIR WINDS

PRESS

GLOUCESTER, MASSACHUSETTS

Text © 2002 Laure Redmond

First published in the USA in 2002 by
Fair Winds Press
33 Commercial Street
Gloucester, MA 01930

10 9 8 7 6 5 4 3 2

Printed and bound in the United States

Cover design by Linda Kosarin
Book design by Leeann Leftwich
Cover photography by Sharon Amestoy

ISBN 1-931412-67-7

*The information in this book is for
educational purposes only. It is not
intended to replace the advice of
a physician or medical practitioner.
Please see your health care provider
before beginning any new health
program.*

DEDICATION

This book is dedicated to my husband, Roger.

Thank you for believing in me as much as I believe in myself and for
restoring my faith in "for better or worse."

You are my forever.

ACKNOWLEDGMENTS

Writing this book has been deeply meaningful.

Although writing a book is a solitary experience, it is impossible to complete without the help of others.

This book has been through many generations of supporters and believers.

Feel Good Naked is a very special title that was born on a terrace in Brooklyn. It was a beautiful summer night. I was describing my original intent to my sister, Sudie, and her husband, Richard. We kept coming back to the word *naked* as the ultimate way to describe someone's physical state. As the three of us excitedly played with the word *naked* we went from feeling good naked to feel good naked. I will never forget how right that moment felt and how lucky I felt to have the support and input of two such brilliant people.

Then I had to sell the concept as a never-been-published-before writer.

My friend Danielle sent me an article from *The New Yorker* about a woman named Jan Miller, who is the ultimate self-help literary agent and owner of Dupree Miller. I remember the note Danielle attached to the article. It read: "Laure—Get your proposal to this woman!"

It took me several months to ready my proposal for Jan. Several people helped me along the way:
Danielle, who spent many hours editing my writing.
Jodi, who spent even more hours editing my writing.
Teresa, who helped me focus and clean my concepts.
Juana, who helped me write my cover letter.
And Roger, who helped me package my materials in a unique, unfor-

gettable way.

I will never forget the phone call I received from Joy Donsky, a wonderful woman who worked with Jan. She called saying that my proposal had been accepted! All of a sudden my ears were clogged and I begged her to repeat what she had just said. She repeated that my proposal had been accepted and that Dupree Miller would be representing *Feel Good Naked*. I hung up the phone, called Roger, and wept with excitement.

Joy passionately championed my concepts, and supported me tirelessly through the process of selling my book. She strategically matched me with a publisher who she trusted would support my journey.

Holly Schmidt at Fair Winds Press has been an energetic match and supporter on this journey. Her excitement and understanding of my goals has been incredible.

Words, stories, and emotions have continued to evolve.

Julie Talbot is the amazing editor I brought onboard to read every word I wrote. Julie is an invaluable editor—bright, patient, organized, thorough, articulate, and creative. I would hate to imagine this intense process without her.

Jonathan Gray, who from the beginning has been a great supporter, friend, and legal counsel for *Feel Good Naked*.

My family: Roger, Christopher, Tyler, Dad, Sudie, and Chris, who have supported me emotionally in an indescribable way. Without whom, I'm nothing.

And last, but never least, I wish to acknowledge and honor women:
Women with whom I have had the privilege to work.
Women whom I have had the honor to understand.
Women who have trusted and believed in my methodologies.

It is with gratitude and respect that I share these heartfelt stories.

TABLE OF CONTENTS

PREFACE: THE AUTHOR'S STORY.

I am a fat woman. Most people would argue that I'm not fat, that I am actually quite trim, and that would be true in the physical sense. But while my body no longer carries the excess weight it once did, I will also always be the same person who was humiliated by my body for many years.

I know the pain of despising my body. And I believe there are thousands of women today who are caught up in the same epidemic I once was. It is rampant, and it is debilitating. And it is not limited to those who are clinically overweight. You'd be astonished how many of the most renowned women in the world—models and actresses whose bodies many would consider perfect—are convinced that they are fat or ugly!

Working with these women, and hearing them echo my own negative body perceptions, proved to me that we need a new language regarding our bodies. Over the past twenty years, I have developed this new language through a ten-step program that has worked beyond my wildest dreams—for me, and for scores of women. It felt important to write this book in order to share my approach with others, in hopes of ending female body hatred.

This program is about finding your way back from body hatred. It's not about diets, or outlandish concoctions, or torturous, excessive exercise regimens. It's about learning to discover and embrace your unique beauty, power, and serenity—about all the wonderful physical things that can happen as a result of a mental transformation. I know because I'm living proof of that transformation.

I was raised in New Orleans, arguably the greatest eating city in the United States. And I ate the most extraordinary food growing up. My grandmother and mother were both well-known gourmet cooks who served tantalizing meals constantly. It was not unusual to eat fried catfish with cheese grits for Sunday breakfast, followed by crabmeat au gratin for lunch, and finishing the day with filet mignon, stuffed potatoes, and creamed spinach. Desserts had wonderful French names like crème caramel and crêpes suzette.

All the women around me, my mother, grandmother, sisters, and their friends, had "normal," well-proportioned figures. Their bodies seemed to tolerate rich foods well, without becoming overweight. In direct contrast was the commotion surrounding my shape. After a few cocktails, my grandmother, Mimi, would whisper loudly, "I'm worried about Lobby's (her nickname for me) weight." My grandmother was a former queen of Mardi Gras, and even the last time I saw her, when she was in her eighties, she carried herself elegantly. In many ways she lived the life of a queen. Queens are not comfortable raising fat granddaughters.

My parents divorced when I was eight. By the time I turned twelve, my weight had climbed forty pounds above the medical charts' recommendation for my age and height, and my mother enrolled me in Weight Watchers. I remember how proud she was when I was awarded the "ten pound" pin in one of our weekly meetings. It was a white circular pin with a bright red number "ten" on it that she quickly attached to the white collar of my school uniform. What an embarrassment having to explain to people the meaning of my pin. I remember my former kindergarten teacher being so inspired by my new figure that she also joined Weight Watchers. It was humiliating seeing her at the weekly meetings.

By the age of thirteen, I had gained back my celebrated ten-pound loss, plus ten more. I was only able to shop at a "special" store called Chubbies and Huskies, and I was ostracized by my peers. I was now at a coed school, where the boys made fun of my body, pulling my skirt up and making mooing sounds. They called me a "heifer," which I was afraid to look up in the dictionary. Sunday afternoons were the only times I saw my father, and we would usually visit an amusement park, followed by dinner at Burger King. I'll never forget asking him over hamburgers and fries what a "heifer" was. It didn't help that I also had frizzy red hair and freckles. My best friend was tall, olive-skinned, and thin with straight hair. Worse still, my two older sisters were the visual opposite of me: statuesque and lean, with perfect dark hair and fabulous features. They looked like my gorgeous mother, who was a New Orleans beauty of Spanish and French origins. I looked like my squinty-eyed, full-cheeked Irish father.

I left New Orleans fourteen and fat, when my mother got remarried and we moved to North Carolina. There I was even more of an outcast. Since preppy clothing was the popular attire—a style not particularly flattering to "heifers"—I stuck to my Chubbies and Huskies wardrobe. I'm not sure which stood out more: my out-of-style clothes, or my rubbing thighs and bulging belly. After I made my first friend, he confided to me that on the first day of eighth grade, everyone thought I was the substitute teacher.

The next year, my mother began fighting a ravaging cancer that quickly took over her body. Her cancer was mean, consuming, and eventually fatal. At the same time, living with my stepfather was becoming increasingly destructive to my development. Besides treating me with constant disdain and verbal abuse, he was especially insensitive to my weight issues, saying things like, "Damn, Laure, with thighs the size of yours, you could play football for the Miami Dolphins." As my sisters became more involved with boyfriends and college, I became more involved with desserts. Food was one of my few reprieves in a world in which I was scared and misunderstood. I got even heavier.

At the end of my tenth-grade year, my mother died. My father was immersed in a high-paced New Orleans bachelor's life; I had little desire to move in with him. And the prospect of continuing to live with my verbally abusive stepfather was no more appealing. I was truly on my own, just three months into my sixteenth year. The decision was made for me to enroll in Saint Mary's, an all-girls boarding school in Raleigh, North Carolina. I was grateful to have a stable place to live after losing my mother and my home. Once again, I was surrounded by women.

I soon learned that the absence of boys may diminish sexual tension, but it does little to cure appearance anxiety. I was shocked at the amount of energy my classmates spent obsessing about their appearances. Thankfully, my roommate Hamer was one of the few girls on campus who was not totally absorbed by her looks. She was comfortable and self-assured. Hamer was a natural beauty; pretty and athletically inclined. She was a jogger, and her body reflected the rewards of her daily exercise commitment.

Shortly after I moved in, Hamer invited me to join her on her daily run. I refused, explaining that I couldn't keep up with her. She casually replied that it wasn't about keeping up, it was about just getting out there and giving it a try. She continued to periodically invite me along; I continued to decline. Finally, on one of those days when I felt down and out and with little to lose, I decided to join her. I will never forget the terror and excitement I felt as Hamer and I started our jog. She was a true inspiration for me, patient and caring as she explained that it wasn't about speed, it was about activating muscles while calming the mind. Pretty wise for a seventeen year old. She slowed her pace way down to my slug's crawl, and I was actually able to jog a full mile. What a feeling of personal accomplishment and power! Yet even more powerful were the mental feelings of confidence, hope, and serenity. I couldn't wait to jog again the next day.

Hamer and I were the only two students at Saint Mary's who jogged regularly. By the end of two years there, my single mile had turned into three. Hamer remained patient with my pace and my side stitches, always sharing the first slow mile with me before breaking away to soar through the woods like a gazelle. We treated our jogging ritual like a religious commitment. Although I was still not thin, I felt different; healthier, more self-assured. My journey into the mind/body connection was beginning.

Despite the traumas I endured before Saint Mary's, several important things happened during the two years that I was there:

- I committed to jogging.
- I realized my life choices were my own.
- I received an excellent education and got accepted to the University of North Carolina at Chapel Hill.
- Hamer became a friend for life.

At Chapel Hill, I discovered the liberation of dancing. Dance classes, dance parties, dancing alone in my dormitory, dancing with men and women. Dancing felt like freedom . . . a break from my anxieties. Jogging felt like an animalistic release . . . a break from my anger and anguish. Portions of my fat finally began to convert into muscle. I weighed more than I ever had, yet I understood that muscle weighs more than fat, which kept me from freaking out. For the first time, I actually began to enjoy looking at myself in the mirror naked. I was enthralled with my changes, inspired by the newfound tightness in my skin. I was also beginning to shop in normal clothing stores without XX's on the size tags.

With my newfound body confidence came a heightened sense of my emerging self. For the first time in my life, I began to feel at ease socially. My enhanced self-esteem made it possible for me to be comfortable in the company of the opposite sex.

During my sophomore year, I began dating Brian, a lacrosse player from Long Island. Brian was an incredible athlete, as well as a kind and caring boyfriend. He introduced me to a community of athletes, which became my surrogate "family." Being a part of his active world enhanced my self-esteem and gave me the confidence to believe I was one of "them." To be able to hang out with this impressive group of jocks, who included me in their weekend workouts, mentally transformed me from feeling like a shameful fat girl into a powerful female. Brian and his teammates gave me the courage to believe that I was physically worthy of their company and respect.

In addition to meeting Brian, and my best female friend, Juana, my most pivotal experience in college was the unexpected discovery of a fabulous exercise studio called Shackelfords. It was the first studio of its type, with exercise classes offered morning, noon, and night, taught by impressive athletic women. I felt connected to the music, to the instructors, to the physical challenges, and to Elizabeth, the owner. The studio provided an environment where I began to thrive. I realized that Elizabeth's job was my dream job. I attended the physically demanding classes at least five times a week, and at the end of my sophomore year, Elizabeth asked me to join the staff. What a great moment! Me—an exercise instructor! "Yes!" I said, "Yes, I will, yes!"

At this point, my physique was beginning to resemble that of an athlete's. Even though I still weighed at least thirty pounds more than the medical charts thought I should, I felt different. My mind-set was becoming more attuned to an athlete's attitude. Oftentimes, complete strangers would ask me if I was a gymnast or swimmer. Nothing made me happier or kept me more motivated to continue my commitment to physical well-being.

Being a teacher at Shackelfords was challenging and intense. I have never worked at anything so demanding, or so rewarding. I realized early on that without question, this was my true calling. Once I became qualified to teach, my classes filled quickly with people of all backgrounds and physical conditioning, including football great Lawrence Taylor, who would take my classes during the off-season to stay in shape. I became seriously driven and motivated to create a lifetime fitness career.

If You Can Make It There, You Can Make It Anywhere

Holidays and summers were spent with my sisters, who were living in New York City. New York felt like home the minute I arrived. The pace, energy, and excitement matched my own, and I relished the diversity of people. The fitness industry was beginning to explode at this time, with New York and Los Angeles at its forefront. On each of my visits to New York, I would take exercise classes in as many studios as I had time for. My favorite classes were at a studio called Body Design By Gilda.

Gilda Marx was a pioneer in the fitness industry. She began her career designing fabulous leotards and spandex outfits and is considered the inventor of aerobics. Gilda was based in Los Angeles, but she owned three New York exercise studios where celebrities flocked by the dozens. Gilda's had the best instructors, the best music, the hottest, most exciting energy. It was not uncommon for me to be taking classes with Brooke Shields, Lisa Hart Black, and other well-known people. The learning pace was demanding and I loved it. I took all of my new moves back to North Carolina to try out on my students, as well as a newfound fantasy: to become a Gilda girl.

On July 7, 1984, my fantasy came true. Upon graduating from college, Gilda hired me to run her Upper West Side studio. No one needed to know that I would have taken the job for free. I had set my sights on working for Gilda and my dream had come true. The "heifer" from New Orleans had finally arrived!

Over the next ten years, I worked hard to create an environment where women felt safe, where celebrities and top models were not harassed, and where everyone who walked in the door was guaranteed a great workout. We were open seven days a week, fifteen hours a day. I was married to the studio, and business was booming. I hired only the best instructors, dancers, actors, and performers who, while waiting for their big break, were willing to contribute several teaching hours a week. My staff included actresses Annabella Sciorra and Connie Britton, and clients often worked out beside Helen Hunt, Andie MacDowell, Mary Stuart Masterson, Tom Cruise, Mary Tyler Moore, Madonna, Kyra Sedgewick, and other luminaries. I was working seventy hours a week and loving every minute of it.

Something extraordinary would happen to me when I taught the classes myself. In retrospect, I would call it a spiritual/physical experience. The honor and opportunity to work with a multitude of people had a profound impact on me. Every time I stood in front of a class, I would remember the pain and isolation of my earlier years, coupled with the exhilaration of my later triumphs. Mixed with these emotions was the excitement of leading a packed house through my moves. I never took this opportunity for granted and always felt deeply connected to my clients. It must have been obvious, because people began to seek me out to work with them privately. As my private practice flourished, along with my group classes, I was asked by ESPN to join the on-air cast of one of their fitness programs.

Aesthetics of the Goddess

One of the most fascinating places in the studio was the women's locker room. After class, everyone would stand around naked waiting to shower and get dressed. My mother, sisters, and roommates had all been modest, and it was wild seeing such a variety of female bodies. I will always remember the time I came face to face with Madonna's nakedness. It was at the same time that her nude image was being exploited by *Penthouse* magazine. I remember thinking it was one of those moments where life imitates art—or was it art imitating life?

Most dramatic was the relief I felt about my own nakedness, in seeing so many other women naked. I could not believe all of the shapes and sizes.

I learned that most women have cellulite, even models. That bosoms naturally droop. That all buttocks sag a bit. That all female bellies stick out a little and that hair grows in many places. Most important was the realization that every woman, for all of her unique and not-so-unique features, is beautiful, especially if she is comfortable in her skin.

Rejuvenating My Path

By 1994, the mega-gym had begun to dominate the fitness scene. My private practice was packed. I closed the studio and allowed a new career to take shape. The actress Mary Tyler Moore and I had developed a three-part exercise video series, which we debuted on the QVC television channel. The response was amazing. I realized early on that if you have a message that you want many people to hear, television is a tremendously powerful vehicle. Today, I continue to work in TV as well as other media, carrying my message of body acceptance and body appreciation to as many people as possible.

Healing Body Hatred

I believe the bottom line for us as women is that if we cringe at the idea of looking at ourselves in the mirror—with or without clothes—how can we possibly present ourselves proudly to the world? I passionately believe that each woman must find a way to change her negative relationship with her body. If she does, she will forever change her life.

Feel Good Naked is the ten-step program for this personal revolution. My ten steps will enable a woman to a) understand what is causing her debilitating body hatred; and b) cure it by escaping damaging mind games, crash diets, and unrealistic exercise regimens. These principles have been used successfully by hundreds of women, including myself, from Hollywood to Manhattan, Boise to Topeka. We have learned to love and appreciate our bodies, which in turn has helped us become stronger, shapelier, and more fit, which in turn has helped us gain confidence and self-esteem. We've become happy with our bodies and, therefore, happier in our lives. This is the fabled "mind-body connection," a term that is used more often than it is understood.

We all know a woman who turns heads whenever she enters a room, even though her legs are not perfect, her body not classically proportioned. And we all wonder, "What does she have that I don't?" My ten-step *Feel Good Naked* program will teach you that her magnetism has everything to do with the way she feels about herself, and little to do with isolated body parts. The woman who turns heads when she enters a room is the woman who follows the *Feel Good Naked* steps.

Today, I weigh anywhere from 130 to 145 pounds. I'm not concerned with minor, natural weight fluctuations, because my life, my body, and my self-image are in a vastly different state than they were when I was fat. Today I am in balance. I love my body, in all its imperfect but unique glory, and my hope is to help others achieve the same serenity.

Throughout this book, you will meet several of my clients, each one different, but success stories all. My hope is that in these case histories, you will be able to see yourself—both in the problems and in the solutions. For purposes of privacy, I have given these women pseudonyms. To further protect the privacy of the individuals involved, certain identifying details have also been changed.

Through my story and the stories of others, you will discover your own path to body self-love. You will find comfort in knowing that you are not alone. And finally, you will learn positive, tangible ways to silence the harshest of critics . . . you. After integrating this program into your life as a companion, and applying my ten steps to your lifestyle, you will finally have the means to become a confident woman. When you walk by, everyone will look. And, more importantly, when you catch sight of yourself in a mirror, you'll gasp with delight. I know it can happen, because it happened to me. And I'm a fat woman.

The Revolutionary *Feel Good Naked* 10-Step Program

Why revolutionary? Because this is the first program whose goal it is to put an end to body hatred, a disease that I believe affects the vast majority of women in America. The ten steps that make up the *Feel Good Naked* program were designed to offer a new way of thinking about, and living in, the unique body you were given.

I've found that women typically come to this program through one of several scenarios:

- they decide they need to lose forty (or twenty or sixty) pounds and want to do it fast
- the imbalances in their lives (regarding time, self-care, food, or other issues) catch up with them in a dramatic "wake-up call"
- their doctor tells them their lifestyle and habits are endangering their health
- their husband or partner leaves them for another woman (not necessarily in that order)

These women have been suffering through pain and problems no one would choose to endure. Yet, I tell them—and I tell you: by not taking control of your own well-being now, you are indeed choosing pain over relief. Deciding to incorporate ten simple and effective steps into your life may not be effort-free, but it is certainly less grueling than the alternative.

The ten *Feel Good Naked* steps are simple, fun, non-intrusive, and they work. Over the past twenty years I have seen hundreds of people affected in profound ways after integrating these concepts into their lives. This book tells the stories of ten of these women, including myself.

Not all ten steps or stories are about the body. Some teach new ways of thinking rather than doing. On any given day, some parts of us need more attention than others. But in order for a human being to thrive, body, mind, and soul must all be nurtured. Used individually or in any combination, the ten steps will lead you to a new relationship with your body, and ultimately to a joyful acceptance of who you are. By embracing the *Feel Good Naked* program, you will put an end to body hatred and you will, quite simply, be a prettier, sexier, more appealing, and happier person—whether or not you're wearing clothes!

The 10-Step *Feel Good Naked* Program

1. Don't deprive yourself. Treat yourself once a week.
If you know that once a week you can pour a bag of M&Ms into your happy mouth, how can you feel deprived? This weekly splurge makes it surprisingly easy to eat healthy, well-balanced meals throughout the rest of the week. Step 1 is the end of dieting as you've come to know it.

2. Drink water, drink water, drink water!
What you've always heard IS TRUE! Drinking two quarts of water a day works minor miracles. It cleans the toxins from your body, keeps you feeling full, and hydrates you from the inside, giving your skin a youthful glow. Furthermore, if you substitute your current consumption of high-calorie sodas with water, and nothing more, you'll probably lose at least five pounds!

3. Watch ten minutes of exercise a day change your face and your life.
Stop being tyrannized by the fear that if you can't work out for an hour, you might as well not work out at all. Pick the cardiovascular activity of your choice and crank up your energy for ten magical minutes. You'll see and feel the results almost immediately in places you would expect, like your abdominal and thigh muscles, and even in places you might not expect such as your neck and face.

4. Schedule fitness appointments in writing each week.

If you don't write it down, you won't do it. It's that simple. So each Sunday before the new week begins, pick at least three days and write down what you plan to do for exercise, whether it is the ten minutes of Step Three, the thirty minutes of Step Eight, or another activity entirely, such as yoga, aerobics, or a walk in the woods. If you carry an appointment book, record your personal appointments there. Commit to this schedule as you would to a business meeting or a baby's feeding—it's every bit as important.

5. Don't stop eating. Stop eating in front of the TV.

Food is a beautiful, glorious part of life and it deserves your full attention. If you eat while you watch TV, you're not giving it that attention, and you're probably overeating! Don't stop eating the foods you love; instead, eat with complete awareness. Turn off the TV and you'll hear what your body is saying—it's telling you how to eat with balance. Balanced eating is an easy, pleasant, guilt-free way to avoid overeating. And overeating makes you fat.

6. Pick an idol and let that person motivate you.

Whether it is your sister, neighbor, Oprah, or Madonna, pick an idol and allow her to inspire you to live a happier life. Put her picture up in your house or office. Change the picture often, so that every time you see it you'll be reminded that she changed, she grew, and you'll be motivated to do the same.

7. Breathe consciously for five minutes every day.

Sit somewhere quiet and breathe deeply and slowly for five minutes each day, in through the nose, out through the mouth, letting your stomach fill with air. This is the most simple, effective way to achieve serenity and neutralize stress, and you can do it anywhere.

8. Take thirty minutes of private time each day.

Use this half-hour any way you choose. Exercise (if the ten minutes in Step Three is not enough), soak in a hot tub, read a book, write in a journal, or simply sit and collect your thoughts. But do it alone. Whether you have to get up at 5:30 A.M. or sneak off to the bathtub after everyone is asleep, carve out this time for yourself and stick to it religiously.

9. Write yourself a love letter once a month.

Though it may seem silly, this is a remarkable way to boost confidence and self-respect. It gradually (and permanently) shifts our focus from self-criticism to love and acceptance. Think of something you really like about yourself—on the surface or more substantial—then write it down. Address it, mail it, and when it arrives, read it—a compliment from the most important person in your life.

10. Stand up straight and tall.

This is an old Louisiana secret that is more powerful than you can imagine. If you practice what self-confidence looks like, you will begin to know what it feels like. My grandmother always told me to stand up straight, pull in my stomach, and smile. She was right. Try it while you're sitting at your desk, standing in line, or walking through the grocery aisles. The response you will get is incredibly fulfilling.

How to Use the 10 Steps

- Begin with Steps One and Two. Practice these steps for a week. The water will cleanse your body while the weekly treat will assure you that you will not feel deprived.

- After one week, add Steps Three and Four. Now you're drinking water, having a treat each week, exercising for ten minutes, and making your body a priority by scheduling the exercise. Do all four steps for three weeks.

- In the fourth week, add Step Five. Do it for a week. At this point, you're cleansing your body, you're thinking about what you eat, you're not depriving yourself, and you're exercising ten minutes a day. You already feel better about yourself, and it's only been one month!

• In week five (the beginning of the second month), add Steps Six and Seven.

• In week six, begin practicing Step Eight.

• In week seven, do Step Nine and continue practicing the steps you've already added to your life.

• In the eighth week, add Step Ten.

• If you are self-motivated, feel free to follow my program in the order of your choice, giving yourself a two-month maximum to incorporate all ten steps.

It's been two months and you've made gentle yet significant changes in your life. Without a doubt, you look and feel different. These steps are designed to give you the wherewithal to believe in yourself, the inner calm to meet roadblocks, and a fantastic feel-good attitude that will signify the end of body hatred and help you face the world with joy and courage.

For Your Information

You will notice that certain issues, concerns, or characteristics come up again and again throughout the different stories, steps, and chapters of this book. In my work, I have found behavioral/psychological patterns such as diet obsession, exercise confusion, warped body image, and lack of self-care to be all too common among women. As a result, I did not shy away from repeating these issues when the stories being told shared similarities. While specific details differ, the commonality is noteworthy.

You will also notice that in each of these ten stories, I offer a "naked" assignment. I encourage you to try these assignments, rituals that will give you a more comfortable and positive experience with the body you live in. They are designed to assist you in your efforts to feel good naked. It's about time that we, as women, claim the birthright of feeling good about our bodies from the inside out. Once you seriously decide to embrace the ten *Feel Good Naked* steps, that decision alone begins to dissipate the distorted self-image you live with. Relief is imminent when there is an honest recognition that a personal change is not only needed, but unavoidable. When you admit that you hate your own naked body, the next simple step is to decide to do something about it.

I refer to the serenity prayer for identifying this process so clearly:
Grant me the serenity to accept the things I cannot change, the courage to change the things I can, and the wisdom to know the difference.

STEP 1

DON'T DEPRIVE YOURSELF. TREAT YOURSELF ONCE A WEEK.

Absence Makes the Appetite Grow Fonder . . . and Fonder . . . and Fonder

Why is it that deprivation seems to go hand-in-hand with being an American woman? It is fascinating to listen to American women greeting each other. A typical conversation often goes something like this:

"Wow—Sally, you look great. What have you done?"

"Well, I have been on the most fabulous diet. In fact, I have lost ten pounds in two weeks and all I had to do was give up all carbohydrates."

At the risk of stereotyping, I believe that conversation would go much differently between two European women. Something more along the lines of:

"Wow—Serena, you look great. What have you done?"

"I have taken a younger lover who feeds me chocolates in bed after we have fabulous sex."

What do we take from this (other than an overwhelming urge to book the next flight to Paris)? That we have much to learn about satisfying our souls and our bodies. And that we must put an end to the dreadful cycle of deprivation that keeps us out of balance both physically and spiritually.

Let's focus for a moment on the notion of giving up carbohydrates. What a crazy—and shortsighted—idea. Not only are carbohydrates a culinary delight, they also provide the body with essential nourishment and energy. Carbohydrates have earned an important place on the famous Food Guide Pyramid for good reason. In *The Encyclopedia of Nutrition and Good Health*, nutrition expert Robert Ronzio (who holds a Ph.D. in biochemistry) writes that without enough carbohydrates in one's diet, the body's metabolism switches into starvation mode, even if ample calories are being consumed through other food groups. In this basic survival state, the body burns muscle as well as fat, undermining any kind of long-term weight loss success. There is simply no scientific evidence that a low carbohydrate diet leads to permanent weight loss.

The truth is, no diet that eliminates an entire food group from your meal choices can ever ultimately benefit your body. Period. Even more convincing than the clinical studies confirming the failure of these weight-loss scams are the myriad examples I've seen among friends and clients. Time and time again I've watched them celebrate a quick weight drop that came by swearing off one food group or another, only to regain the weight—and more—as their metabolism was thrown off base. Because muscle burns more energy (calories) than fat, it is not beneficial to lose muscle. Furthermore, when you gain the weight back, you gain back fat, not lost muscle, which causes your body to look worse than before the diet. Ultimately, the disservice of depriving your body of balanced food choices always comes back to haunt you, while also slowing down your body clock or metabolism.

Yet in our obsessive quest for the shortest route to weight loss, we ignore the risks and buy into the promise, at any price. And, as the multibillion-dollar diet product empire will attest, I do mean any price.

What the promise is really selling, however, is deprivation—not salvation. And therein lies the problem. By depriving ourselves of a food we love, we become so preoccupied with what we're not getting that we binge our brains out the moment that particular food walks back into our lives—which it inevitably does.

One of the saddest deprivation memories from my fat childhood was Christmas 1974. I looked so overweight to my mother and grandmother that they decided it would be best if I was locked away in the playroom to make paper ornaments during the annual bake-fest, so as not to tempt my large body with samples of pralines, heavenly hash, and sugar sand tarts. I'll never forget the horrible sense of isolation I felt when the laughter, hushed whispers, and sweet smell of heated dark chocolate wafted into the playroom; the sense of urgency I experienced when my eldest sister sneaked in with warm fingerfuls of the freshly baked heavenly hash. I felt utterly desperate licking her fingers for dear life.

Vive la Différence

As I mentioned earlier, my most notable teachers in regard to enjoying food have been European women. Generally speaking, they are exquisite creatures, and I have studied them with fascination and respect. They know how to present themselves to the world with an unapologetic sense of self-pride. It is extremely powerful—and utterly sexy.

What's more, they don't just enjoy food—they worship it. Yet for some reason, Europeans obviously have less trouble with their weight than Americans. Barely 8 percent of French people are overweight, compared to 30 percent of Americans. There's even a name for it: the French paradox.

I believe the secret of the paradox lies precisely in the notion, and tradition, of worshipping food. It's all about quality instead of quantity, about treating a meal as the day's most pleasurable and relaxing event. Every morsel is a revelation, and no savory taste or texture is denied. Yet bingeing is very rare in Europe; they don't need to stuff large quantities of food into their mouths all at once since they allow themselves full culinary pleasures when enjoying a meal. Notice I said "full"—not "excessive." Variety is embraced, gluttony is not. A simple meal at a French bistro might include a creamy leek and potato soup, steak frites (steak and french fries), a green salad topped with a round of warm goat cheese, and a caramelized apple tart—accompanied by a glass or two of wine, a basket of crusty French bread, and espresso with small squares of bittersweet chocolate.

Yet the portions of each of these choices would look tiny to most Americans. Again, the emphasis is on the intensity and nuance of taste, not on how many times a person can return to the buffet bar.

Europeans also generally eat three meals a day, at about the same time every day, making it unnecessary to gorge on high-calorie snacks in between. Taking the time to enjoy three satisfying meals every day is a huge key to successful weight loss. There is no impulse to binge on snacks when you know you will be eating well again in just a few hours. Remember, nutritionally-empty, highly processed snacks will make you fat. Balanced, tasty meals made from whole foods will keep you healthy, and contribute to a lean and consistent body weight.

Is Life without Chocolate Really Worth Living?

I believe that treating ourselves is one of life's great pleasures, especially when that treat is a true gift to our spirit and not a detriment to our body. Which means honoring ourselves with purpose and in moderation. Accepting what we enjoy and incorporating it into our lives in a healthy, balanced manner—even if it's fattening—helps to ease the anxiety of fearing that we will never again be allowed the pleasures that we crave.

Every client I work with has a "food thing," but then, most likely, so does every person I pass on the street. We all have food issues. What I can promise you is that diets—and especially diets that exclude or eliminate certain foods—do not work. Save your money, time, and metabolism, because no matter how much weight falls off at the beginning of a diet, at some point, we all return to the foods we love. And that's as it should be.

I love chocolate. I will always love chocolate. Chocolate makes me happy. Thankfully, I can enjoy chocolate in moderation without feeling guilty. There is no reason to feel bad about something that makes you feel good. Eating what you like—within reason—is about blessing yourself with choices. Choices grant us freedom. (Step Five will teach you more about moderation while eating and how to know when your stomach is full.)

The greatest truth I have learned about eating is that food can be, in fact should be, a wonderful celebration of life. After all, it keeps our bodies going, which makes it the essence of life. Our bodies are our very own precious engines and food is the fuel that energizes these engines. Just think, if you owned a beautiful, rare sports car, you would never put low-octane gas in it. You would fill the engine each time with the best gas available. Your body is that rare sports car. The key is to fill it adequately with the best foods possible. And when the tank is full, to stop pumping the gas.

Instead of thinking of your favorite foods as a "weakness" or "downfall" to be shamefully banished, hold them high on a pedestal. Give them their due respect as an important, positive part of your life, but a part that, like most pleasures, should be enjoyed in moderation if the magic is going to hold. Then look forward to reveling in those treats once a week. Once you successfully incorporate this weekly treat into your life, you will hopefully discover that, like the French, you are capable of enjoying a small treat each day. Yet in order to go from a weekly treat to a daily treat, you must be able to enjoy food in moderation and with control. If you feel tempted to always eat more than a sampling of your favorite tastes or to lose control and binge, stick with the weekly treat.

What are the "rules" for your weekly treat? It can be anything: chocolate, barbecued potato chips, cookie dough, pot roast—or any combination thereof. The only rule is that your treat cannot exceed 500 calories. I've found that anything less leaves you feeling cheated, any more runs the risk of leading to bingeing.

Not sure how to compute the calories? Most packaged foods have calorie counts on the labels called Nutrition Facts. Homemade dishes are a little more difficult, but can still be calculated by adding up each of the ingredients separately. Obviously, you will be able to adjust the quantity of your treat based on the total number of calories. You may choose a low-fat version with fewer calories in order to have more to eat . . . or you may decide that flavor is everything, and go with a small portion of something decadently rich. The choice is yours. To help yourself avoid bingeing, especially if you have to buy or make more than your 500-calorie allotment, measure out the exact amount you will eat before you take a single bite—and freeze the rest or give it to your neighbor. Yes, even if it's an entire cake you've just baked. Yes, even if it's two-thirds of a box of Captain Crunch®. Frankly, it's a small price to pay for avoiding the temptation that can derail your goals.

Before I introduce you to Erin, I want to divulge a secret that became the foundation of her success. It is a secret that the thriving weight-loss industry doesn't want you to know, but that doesn't make it any less true. There are no magic pills or secret formulas for weight loss. You may be seduced by the false promises of diets and trendy weight-loss programs, however, those options only prove disastrous in the long run. To be satisfied with your body is a process. It is an education that requires a shift in the way you see yourself, striking a sane balance between what and how you eat and your activity level. That's it. It's that simple. The sooner you learn this basic truth, the happier you will be.

Thankfully, Erin learned this lesson in her twenties, which saved her from many decades of deprivation and failure. But it's never too late to learn. Hopefully Erin's story will help inspire you to never deprive yourself again.

Instead, embrace your three meals with balance and grace, knowing that your favorite treat is always just around the corner.

Erin's Story

Erin started coming to my exercise studio while she was in college. She is a native Manhattanite who left New York City to go to college. However, the minute she arrived home for holidays or summer breaks, she was at the studio, ready to work out. Many times, I would see her in class twice a day. Erin seemed to live for exercise.

Her shyness is what I most remember in the beginning. Erin is from a famous New York family and she often ducked her head when saying hello or goodbye, eager to work out hard and avoid being recognized. My experience with celebrities at my studio taught me this language early on; most cherish their exercise time as a rare escape from the limelight. Yet the contagious energy and electricity that filled our classes made even the most camera-shy willing to brave open classes of as many as forty people. Erin's defense was to simply appear and disappear with as little fanfare as possible.

One day, before class, I overheard Erin talking to a friend about her constant knee pain. I jumped into the conversation, offering to keep an eye on her body placement during class to see if I noticed anything that might be contributing to her knee pain. Sure enough, during class, I noticed several body alignment issues that could cause knee problems. After class, I shared my observations with Erin, who was not only grateful for my interest, but eager to know if we could work together privately. We booked our first appointment, and I asked her to bring me a journal of everything she had eaten over the past week. Erin agreed with a look that somehow combined curiosity, discomfort, and relief.

Erin is one of my favorite success stories because when we began our private sessions, she was one of the most damaged women I had ever worked with. She had many negative body issues, numerous psychological food issues, and no female role models. Yet under all of this was a woman begging to be freed of those compulsions, exhausted by the amount of energy her neuroses required, and most important, open, receptive, and willing to make changes in her life in order to be a happier person. These are some of the most important steps for self-empowerment . . . you must have a willingness to be completely honest about your choices and habits, and a desire to change the things that you can.

Erin was well prepared for our first meeting, with a detailed food journal in hand and an excitement that was deeply touching to me. I was shocked to learn how little she ate on a regular basis. Even more startling was the litany of food sensitivities she had, and the forbidden foods she explained were off-limits. She told me several stories of times when she had eaten the wrong food and ended up in the hospital with digestive problems. As well, there were stories of eliminating almost every food known to man with the goal of losing the twenty extra pounds that she found impossible to shed. Erin hoped I could help her lose those pounds, as well as the persistent knee pain that was making her workouts so painful.

With all due respect to Erin's medical problems, I had the gnawing sense that her severe eating limitations were largely self-imposed. I remember silently thinking, how do we do this to ourselves? Why don't men do this? What would Erin's life be like without all of these concerns?

Helping Erin lose the weight and the knee pain required going back to her childhood and rewriting her script for being a happy woman. There were two main influences in Erin's life that she needed to fully understand and forgive in order to heal her demons . . . her mother and her stepmother.

All women are indoctrinated into the female world through the experiences of their mothers. If our mothers are not at peace with their bodies or comfortable in their skin, how can they pass on comfort and confidence to us? It is a sad legacy. Our fathers, on the other hand, inevitably teach us as women how the opposite sex will interpret, perceive, and respond to us. As a result, both heavily influence our female foundation.

In that regard, my father was a healthier influence on me than my mother. I can largely attribute the development of positive aspects of my body image to him, though he was ignorant of his power. My mother generally made me feel fat and unattractive. Conversely, my father's comments were always affirmative, and around him—even as a child—I felt beautiful. When it came time to eat, my mother would suggest that I limit my intake of sweets and high-fat foods. My father, on the other hand, never censored my quantities or choices. To the contrary, he wanted to ensure that I was content and had had enough to eat. This was the first time I realized that when food is comfortably offered and made available for consumption, it removes some of the intrigue and allure of overeating or bingeing.

An example of this was the difference between my mother's and father's kitchens. At my mother's house, sweets were tucked away. The cruel thing was, I knew they were there, because they would suddenly appear when guests stopped by. Sometimes I would catch my mom having a cookie or a slice of pound cake, but there was no evidence of where it had come from, and she never readily offered these treats to me. It only made me obsess more about the forbidden fruit I was missing. On the other hand, at my father's house, sweets were never singled out as "bad." They were offered and visually available along with a wonderful variety of other foods. I ate what I wanted at his house. As a result, I found that I rarely binged or obsessed over desserts at my father's—even though they were much more accessible. It was one of my first lessons in the backlash of deprivation.

For Erin, the influence of her mother and stepmother had not been positive with regard to food. Both had lived several lifetimes of diets. One week it might be the grapefruit diet. A different week, the mango diet. Erin's childhood meals were defined by what these two neurotic women would be eating—or not eating—any given week. Erin was constantly told to watch what she ate. Even before she started high school, she had learned dieting as a means for managing her weight.

On the other hand, Erin's father had a celebratory view of eating and relished the opportunity to share good food with the people he cared about. So while Erin was learning from the women in her family to avoid most foods, her father would be eager to sit down and share a huge, bountiful meal with her. The mixed messages were too much. By the time Erin and I met, her body was so confused and deprived that it had begun to react with the symptoms of food intolerance.

In our second meeting, I told Erin the two changes that I thought she needed to make:
1. She needed to eat more.
2. She needed to work out less.

You can imagine her response. She thought I was kidding, and she hoped that I wasn't.

I explained. Besides not producing the desired long-lasting weight-loss control Erin hoped for, her severe calorie-reduction diets had wreaked all sorts of physical havoc with her body. Consuming too few calories (fewer than 1000 calories a day for a woman) for more than a few weeks signals our bodies to go into starvation mode, which causes us to burn muscle tissue as well as fat. This in turn can result in the loss of heart muscle tissue. It can also affect joint and limb function, as with Erin's knee pain. Additionally, decreased food intake lowers our metabolic rate—the rate at which we burn calories—so that the body requires less food to maintain the same weight. When the diet is abandoned due to poor results, and regular eating is resumed, the metabolic rate is still lower—so weight is actually regained even faster than prior to the diet. Erin's dieting had robbed her body of many essential nutrients and vitamins that help us function optimally.

I comforted her with the assignment of eating three nourishing meals a day. I also told her that once a week she could have 500 calories worth of anything she craved that was normally considered a "bad" food.

At first, it was difficult for Erin to allow herself to eat three full meals a day. She felt scared that she would gain weight, and she admitted to having no idea what to eat for those meals. The truth was, her weight was well within acceptable guidelines, and was the least of her worries. To help get her started on a healthier diet, I gave her some suggestions, based on the foods that help me feel—and function—at my best. My system is no secret; it's a balanced approach that emphasizes variety and is based on the basic Food Guide Pyramid and dietary guidelines set by the U.S. Department of Agriculture.

These guidelines recommend that each of us eat daily:
Six to eleven servings of bread, cereal, rice, and pasta
Three to five servings of vegetables
Two to four servings of fruit
Two to three servings of meat, poultry, fish, dry beans, eggs, and nuts
Two to three servings of dairy products
Fats and sweets sparingly

Scanning this list, Erin blurted out, "There's no way I can eat this much in one day." She was also concerned about trying foods that had caused digestive discomfort in the past. I told her to initially focus on the minimum number of servings in each food group, and to find alternatives within each group to specific foods she had had difficulties with. For instance, broccoli and cauliflower were problem foods for her, but as I pointed out, that still left dozens of other vegetables to try. I also gave her some sample meals that I enjoy. While I try to keep my total caloric intake for the day to around 1500–1800 calories, that may be not enough, or too much, for someone else. And I am not compulsive about calories. Like the French, I try to concentrate on the sensory experience of enjoying each bite, and let my body tell me when I'm full. A good book about eating smart and joyfully is Oprah Winfrey and Bob Greene's *Make the Connection*.

Please understand that my first priority for Erin was getting balanced nutrition back into her diet, so the sample meals that follow are not intended for weight loss. I am able to maintain my weight in an acceptable zone by eating meals like these. However, they could serve as a balanced basis for a weight-loss program if you simply reduce the portions.

Always check with your physician before embarking on any new food regimen.

Sample Breakfast Options:

1. One medium-sized fresh orange, one poached egg, one slice whole wheat toast with a pat of butter, coffee with skim milk (325 calories)

2. Bran flakes cereal with one cup skim milk, eight ounces orange juice, one cup fresh strawberries, tea (370 calories)

3. Three pancakes (4" diameter), pat of butter, one fresh peach sliced on top of pancakes, eight ounces skim milk (400 calories)

4. One cup plain yogurt, one cup oatmeal, one-half cup blueberries mixed in with yogurt or oatmeal, eight ounces grapefruit juice (485 calories)

Sample Lunch Options:

1. One cup navy-bean soup, tomato sandwich on two slices of toasted whole wheat bread with one tablespoon of Dijon mustard and leaf of lettuce, one-half cup cole slaw, one pear (435 calories)

2. Salad Nicoise with tuna, hard-boiled egg, olives, and other veggies; fresh apple, eight ounces skim milk (535 calories)

3. Smoked salmon on bagel with two tablespoons cream cheese, bunch of green grapes, one-half cup baby carrots (485 calories)

4. Grilled or broiled chicken breast, one-half cup steamed broccoli, two medium chocolate chip cookies, tea (550 calories)

Sample Dinner Options:

1. Flank steak, one ear of corn, one pat of butter, salt to taste, green salad with one tablespoon dressing, one cup fresh berries (425 calories)

2. Grilled halibut steak basted with lemon and olive oil, three-fourths cup brown rice with chopped green pepper, two broiled tomato slices with dill, one-half cup raspberry sorbet (620 calories)

3. One and one-half cups linguine with three tablespoons pesto sauce, sliced carrots and green pepper with one tablespoon dressing, two slices French bread dipped in olive oil, two-inch slice of cheesecake, tea (870 calories)

4. Stir-fry beef with mushrooms, onions, and red peppers, cooked in olive oil; sourdough roll, pat of butter, steamed asparagus, slice of apple pie (850 calories)

If you enjoy a glass or two of wine with lunch and/or dinner, add an additional 100 calories per glass.

Because of my very active lifestyle, it is not uncommon for me to need one or two mini-meals between breakfast and lunch or lunch and dinner. Don't confuse these mini-meals with the empty, non-nutritious calories of many traditional "snack" foods. Mini-meals consist of healthy, nutrition-packed foods. Three of my favorite choices are:

1. Fresh fruit mixed with plain nonfat yogurt
2. A nutritious energy bar (check the Nutrition Facts label to make sure they really are nutritious, and not just sugar treats in disguise)
3. Baby carrots or other easy-to-munch vegetables

Also, I drink at least ten glasses of water every day (Step Two).

More Is Less

In the beginning, Erin feared that her new way of eating included too much food. But she began to trust that eating three meals a day was essential for maintaining an appropriate weight. While she did indeed gain a few pounds at first (while her metabolism was still in its "starvation" mode), slowly but surely her metabolism began to shift into a more productive state as she combined her new diet with a regular exercise schedule. Interestingly, she discovered that she didn't need to lose as much weight as she thought she would to feel good about her body—a ten-pound loss turned out to be plenty.

Erin continued to record her daily food intake in a journal. Looking back at weeks past, she soon realized that before she began eating three meals a day, many nutritionally-lacking foods such as pretzels, cookies (albeit non-fat), sodas, and muffins had become a large part of her daily diet. In fact, snacks had taken the place of meals for her.

Once she weaned herself off the snacks and began eating three full meals a day, she found that her body was so satisfied that she did not even want to snack anymore. As well, she noticed a huge increase in her energy level.

When I asked about her once-a-week splurge, she admitted that, like me, chocolate seemed to be her number-one pick. Yet it was only now, without the desperation that had come with bingeing in the past, that she was able to truly appreciate the taste of this delicious indulgence. Before, chocolate had been so forbidden that when she ate it, she would gobble it down, barely able to enjoy the pleasure, having been taught to feel so guilty.

To deepen her appreciation of this treat, I suggested something radical: that she eat her chocolate in the nude. She thought I was joking, but I explained that it was important for her to make a mindful connection between her body and the enjoyable, positive gift she was treating herself to; to replace the negative relationship she'd always perceived between her body and food. Savoring her chocolate treat was a self-affirming celebration, and I wanted her to include her body as part of that celebration. Erin reported back to me that eating her chocolate naked made her not only feel like a movie star, but that it made her eat slower and more deliberately, truly appreciating each morsel.

Pain—No Gain

When Erin and I began working together, she was as obsessed about working out as she was about dieting. She had convinced herself that she needed multiple workouts every day in order to avoid gaining weight—which, coupled with her food deprivation, caused her body to begin to break down. She had lost precision and control in her movements, and her muscles, joints, and ligaments were being overworked and undernourished. Each time she took class, the supportive tissue surrounding her knees was being strained, which was causing chronic pain.

Gradually and with admirable dedication, Erin followed my advice. She tapered her workout schedule from nine workouts a week to five. By the fourth week, she was eating three full meals a day—and wondering how she had gotten so far away from what her body truly needed. That's not to say there weren't difficult times, of course, days when she was tempted to skip a meal and work in an extra exercise class. However, she had committed to the program and gradually began reaping the rewards of a life that balances healthy eating with moderate but regular activity. Within several weeks, her knee pain was gone.

Today, ten years later, Erin is in the prime of her life and excels in the many areas of her busy schedule. She is about to be married to a wonderful man. Interestingly, Erin no longer suffers from food sensitivities. She follows the *Feel Good Naked* lifestyle with ease and pleasure. Old habits die hard, however, and she still catches herself being tempted by certain diets, but then it only takes a few seconds for her to separate the past from the present, and to realize that diets will only bring her heartache and failure.

Erin eats three healthy meals a day and continues to keep a food journal. She exercises in moderation. Her weight fluctuates slightly, between five and ten pounds less than when she first came to me—far from the twenty pounds she thought she needed to lose. Yet that weight feels right to her now. Her life is in balance. We recently agreed that instead of succumbing to thoughts of shedding an extra ten pounds for the wedding, she would visualize the beautiful, healthy body she has created, showcased by a wedding dress.

Summary:

Erin's issues were all about deprivation and obsessive-compulsive behavior. Because she had received such damaging, mixed messages about food as a young woman, she had no idea how to eat healthily. Her metabolism had been seriously altered by dieting, which made it difficult for her to function normally, let alone lose weight. As well, she had ended up in the hospital several times from her body's adverse reactions to certain foods.

Erin was taught early in her life to cut out all "bad" foods or she would be fat and unattractive. Yet all the deprivation did was bring on desperate bingeing episodes, followed by desperate overexercise to counter the overeating. Without nutritional resources to fuel her workouts, her knees began to suffer.

Once she started keeping a food journal, Erin could see how unbalanced her diet was. Ten years later, she continues to keep a diary as a gauge of how well she's eating. This written record will give you an acute awareness of your relationship with food and will encourage you to eat healthier. If you see it written down on paper, you cannot deny or ignore your reality.

By committing to a balanced, nutritious eating plan, Erin learned to focus on the quality and variety of foods she ate, not just the quantity. By eating more (and more nutritiously) and exercising less, her injuries were able to heal and her body was able to function more effectively.

Being able to look forward to a well-deserved food treat once a week took away her negative association with "bad" foods, and made it easier for her to stick to healthy choices the rest of the week.

Step One is all about learning balance. Living a balanced, moderate life is a major key to being happier with your body—and in your body. As Erin learned, it is essential to eat three nutritious meals a day with a weekly 500-calorie indulgence of whatever food your heart desires. If you know you get to splurge once a week, you will be encouraged to remain balanced with your meal choices for the rest of the week.

STEP 2

DRINK WATER, DRINK WATER, DRINK WATER!

Why Are "Soft" Drinks So Hard to Give Up?

Yesterday I was walking with one of my clients. Bright, lively, and opinionated, Jane is a far different person today than when I first met her three years ago. Then she was an overly self-conscious creature of habit who had little awareness of what went into her body every day. She was by some measures slightly overweight, but not nearly so much as she perceived.

Among the lifestyle changes that fueled Jane's transformation was something so simple it is often glossed over in discussions of fitness and health. Yet few other adjustments alter our body processes so fundamentally. And that's developing a close personal relationship with water.

Jane used to have a major Big Gulp® (super-sized self-serve grocery soda) habit. She lives with two roommates who are confirmed sodaholics. When I first asked her why she preferred soda pop over good old-fashioned water, she started waxing poetically about "the bubbles, the fizz, the satisfying feeling" she got from her daily doses of soft drinks. I realized she could have been describing the experience of drinking champagne. Jane told me that not only did her roommates drink soda constantly, so did everyone in her office, "almost unconsciously."

From this revelation, it would be easy to assume that if more people were conscious about the remarkable advantages of water, and the unhealthy effects of soft drinks, they'd be more willing to switch. Unfortunately, it's not that simple. Besides the addictive qualities of the caffeine found in many sodas, our bodies also become attached to the taste and texture of what we drink. Jane suffered through two weeks of horrible headaches and fatigue when she stopped drinking Big Gulps® everyday. She could not believe how dependent her body had become on the ingredients in soda pop. She even compared giving up soda to the anguish of quitting smoking.

Yet, the infinite, almost miraculous, benefits associated with substituting water for other drinks are enough to give even the most die-hard soda fan reason to reconsider.

Water Is the Celebrity Secret

How many photos have you seen of celebrities who happen to be carrying a water bottle? It's no accident. This is a great lesson to learn from those whose lives depend on looking and feeling good.

How can water help your body, mind, and spirit? Let us count the ways.
- weight loss
- reduced appetite
- flatter stomach, less bloating
- prettier skin
- better sleep
- fewer headaches

- better soft tissue function (muscles, tendons, etc.)
- more energy, less sluggishness
- money saved

People who start consciously drinking more water are often surprised to find that they lose five pounds within the first two weeks, without doing anything else to lose weight! The reason is that without proper hydration, the body retains fluids. That's right—the less water we drink, the more we retain. To shed the unnecessary weight of retained water, we must drink more water! Plus, drinking ample amounts of water also works as a natural appetite suppressant, so we consume fewer calories.

Drinking water also cleanses and nourishes your system, helping your kidneys function optimally, and ridding your body of waste. A specific side effect of this process that you will notice at first is frequent trips to the bathroom which will lessen as your body adjusts to processing greater amounts of water. You will also notice less bloating in the abdominal region (especially if you were drinking a lot of soda), less swelling in your extremities if you have been suffering from fluid retention, and more comfortable fitting clothes.

Drinking lots of water gives the skin a healthier, more radiant appearance. Recently, a popular talk show featured an anti-aging expert who was offering simple hints for looking younger. His number one tip? Drinking eight glasses of water a day. Drinking sodas and coffee—and not enough water—dehydrates your skin, making your face look parched, heavily lined, and older, as if you'd stayed out in the sun too long. Water, on the other hand, feeds your skin with much-needed hydration, giving skin cells plumpness and resiliency.

Having trouble sleeping? Plagued by headaches? Many of my clients experience a profound improvement in their quality of sleep and both the number and severity of headaches when they substitute water for their soda/coffee habit.

As for saving money, grab a pencil, piece of paper, and calculator right now. Add up how much money you spend a day on soda or coffee. Now figure out how much you spend a week, a month, a year. Water is free, or at least significantly less, even if you drink bottled water. Fantasize about how you will spend the money if you agree to start drinking water instead of costly beverages. Then create a jar or bank where you place the savings each day that you would have spent on coffee or soda. At the end of a year, treat yourself to your fantasy purchase.

How much water is enough? Most experts recommend drinking eight eight-ounce glasses of water each day. I personally try to drink ten glasses. You don't have to start at that level, though. Give your body a chance to adjust by working up to sixty-four ounces a day over a week or so.

Retraining Your Taste Buds

Okay, so water is good for you. But do you really have to give up that diet soda? Can't you just add water to your drink line-up?

Soft drinks are at best non-nutritious and at worst damaging to your body. They are filled with all kinds of ingredients that can cause abdominal bloating, retention of fluids, and ironically, dehydration. For the heck of it, read a soda can sometime. You will be shocked at how many artificial, hard-to-pronounce words make up the list of ingredients. What in the world is gum arabic? Brominated vegetable oil? Phenylalanine? These words all came off the side of a can of diet soda. If you were a fish, would you rather swim in large, syrupy vats of unpronounceable concoctions, or a clear mountain stream? Think of your inner "machinery" as that fish.

It was the mindful realization that I was actually putting this stuff into my body that motivated me to kick my soft-drink habit. I remember the moment vividly. I was waiting for a friend to meet me and to bide the time, I absentmindedly began reading the ingredients on my can of soda. The more I read, the more horrified I became. Please understand, I was no radical health nut, but I felt grossed out in that moment. I reread the can to confirm that I had read it completely the first time. That was it! I threw away the unfinished soda and never looked back.

Breaking any detrimental habit—whether it's cigarettes, soda pop, or some other vice—means living through an uncomfortable adjustment period. If your palate is used to the tingle of soft-drink fizz, or to the distinct flavor of cola, then suddenly switching to water will feel less satisfying. As Jane remembers, "For those first few days, water is like a non-taste." It helps to accept that the first two weeks without your habitual substance will be hell. But after those initial two weeks, your taste buds will begin to discern the quenching, satisfying properties of water as appealing in their own right. More important, your entire body will begin to feel better. Jane confirmed that by her third week without soft drinks, her skin looked brighter, her stomach felt flatter, and her headaches, lethargy, and abdominal discomfort had disappeared. These positive differences motivated her to keep chugging water instead of soda pop.

I have reached for water instead of soft drinks for many years now. But as an experiment, I recently tried a can of soda pop after a sweaty workout. My thirst was huge, so I popped the top and started to guzzle. Scarcely had I taken my first, wanting sip when I recoiled, spitting it out on the spot. It was nasty. All my tongue got was a harsh dose of chemicals. After twenty years without soda, my body craved what it knew: water.

To Ease the Transition

Here are several soft-drink substitutes to help ease the way (in addition to the increased water intake):

- homemade iced tea with a squeeze of lemon and fresh mint (forget the bottled variety, which has as many artificial ingredients as soda).
- iced coffee with milk or soy milk, vanilla, and a bit of sugar to taste.

- seltzer water with a little cranberry juice or orange juice.
- homemade lemonade with fresh peppermint.
- any 100 percent fruit juice on ice (forget the bottled varieties that are not pure juice).

Good to the Last Drop

I chuckle at the memory of a client, Mary, who creatively suggested that she would like to substitute her daily intake of water with coffee, since coffee is made with water. I explained to her that, regretfully, this would not work. Coffee is not a substitute for water, nor is any other beverage that contains water.

Coffee has practically reached cult status over the past ten years, as high-quality coffee has become readily available. On street corners and in airports, we can now order a "skinny double cappuccino," and even the most novice clerk nods knowingly. I find it challenging to remember the world before Starbucks®. Imagine: creating a national chain of stores that provides us with easy access to one of the most habit-forming stimulants in the world. On page sixty-eight in *The Encyclopedia of Nutrition and Good Health*, caffeine usage is said to be "linked to most, though not all, attributes of addiction (chemical dependency), including craving and withdrawal symptoms during abstinence." Small wonder soft drinks with caffeine are much tougher to give up than those without.

Should coffee be permanently banished from your diet, never to be seen again? With respect to the *Feel Good Naked* lifestyle, I will never advise you to give up anything that you enjoy if it doesn't pose serious health threats. However, I will constantly aim to teach you balance. Certainly coffee can be abused, like soft drinks. Again from page sixty-eight in *The Encyclopedia of Nutrition and Good Health*, "moderate consumption of caffeine-containing foods does not seem to be harmful for the average adult. Most healthy individuals can tolerate 200 to 300 mg or two to three cups of coffee a day of caffeine as a mild stimulant. Side effects of excessive caffeine (800 mg or more) include anxiety, sleeplessness, agitation, shortness of breath, irregular heartbeat, nausea, heartburn and headaches."

Coffee should never be used as a substitute for water. But I have always professed that up to two cups of coffee a day does little to endanger a healthy, balanced diet. Better yet, try adopting the ritual of drinking tea instead of coffee. Over the years, I have heard many nutritionists suggest that if you must have caffeine, caffeinated tea is better for your body than coffee. A cup of green tea can provide as much vitamin C as half a cup of orange juice. Both black and green tea contain antioxidants, which may work as anti-cancer agents. And tea consumption has also been linked to a lowered risk of dying from heart disease.

In short, one of the least complex, least expensive, and most effective things you can do on your path to a balanced, healthy body is simply to drink more water, fewer soft drinks, and a minimal amount of coffee. Certainly, it's more appealing than dieting or plastic surgery. And considerably less painful. Kathy's story reinforces all of these important points.

Kathy's Story

Kathy is a successful forty-five-year-old career woman who is married with two daughters. When she sought me out, she was heavier than she had been at any time in her life—fifty pounds heavier than her self-determined "ideal" weight. The year before, when she was forty pounds overweight, she had tried Weight Watchers. Before that, at thirty pounds too many, she had joined a health club, hired a private trainer, and taken two exercise classes. And back when she was only twenty pounds overweight, she had consulted with a nutritionist to learn how to eat right.

Kathy could not figure out what had happened. All she could admit was that she needed a new method, a new program, a new lease on herself. Kathy needed to renew her faith in her own body; she had none left. She was not confident that she had ever had genuine faith in her body.

During our first telephone conversation, I asked Kathy how many years she could remember feeling self-conscious in her body.

"Forty." (Kathy is only forty-five years old.)
How many clothing sizes had she had as an adult?
"Five sizes—eight, ten, twelve, fourteen, sixteen."
How much money had she invested in trying to change her body?
"Um . . . well . . . let's see . . . gee, probably over $10,000."

I wanted to know, after so many varied approaches, why she had sought me out? She said she had been motivated by her neighbor Judy, who had worked with me for years. Through hard work and an inspiring reversal of her lowly self-image, Judy had changed everything about her body that she once hated. For a number of years, she has maintained her ideal weight without dieting, and more importantly, is no longer obsessed with any of her previous body issues. The dramatic transformation had not been lost on Kathy, whose family often joins Judy's for backyard barbecues. Judy had talked about her *Feel Good Naked* experience. Kathy decided it was her last chance to help herself.

I also wanted to know: why now? Kathy answered that she could see how her own warped body issues were beginning to damage her daughters. She could no longer ignore the fear that she was passing along a horrible legacy of female body self-hatred. Kathy was also scared that her healthy, lean, active husband might be losing interest in her. He had started coming home later in the evenings, and had recently joined a running team that met on weekends and included several active, attractive women. For the first time in their ten-year relationship, she sensed that he could be interested in having an affair. In some ways, Kathy didn't blame him. She had practically given up all hope for herself—why shouldn't he?

My first counsel to Kathy was that having the courage to take that first step again—especially after experiencing repeated failures—was by far the hardest part, and that she had already made a great stride.

Kathy showed up for her first appointment clutching a diet soda. She drank the entire can within our first fifteen minutes together, and I learned that she consumed at least a six-pack of diet soda a day, often more.

When we discussed her goals, she said she needed to lose at least fifty pounds, and she also wanted to flatten her abdominal region. Like many mothers I work with, she claimed that her stomach had never been the same since having children, especially the area right below her belly button.

Over the course of our conversation, I learned that Kathy suffered from other physical problems: intestinal bloating and gas, mood swings, fatigue—all of which I knew could be attributed to her soda habit. By the end of my initial meeting with Kathy, I felt she needed not only a change in beverage choices, but also a cardiovascular outlet, such as walking, and an education in the joyful experience of balanced eating. The moment I mentioned balanced eating, she grew uncomfortable, saying that she knew I would tell her not to eat chocolate, cookies, or frozen yogurt (her favorites). I explained emphatically that she would be able to continue eating her favorite foods (Step One), however, I wanted to teach her how to eat with a conscious mind (Step Five).

Her interest was piqued. She joked that this plan sounded too sane to be true.

What about "no pain, no gain"? I explained that the goal of the *Feel Good Naked* program is to live a happier, more balanced life in which she will become passionate about picking healthy choices for herself. She didn't need to be reminded of how stressful dieting is. However, I said, I wasn't letting her off scot-free: her first assignment was to start cutting back on her daily six cans of diet soda. I wanted her to give up a can a day over the next week, until she was down to only one soda a day. I suggested that she always carry a big bottle of water with her, and that when she felt her soda withdrawals kicking in, she should guzzle bottles of the water until she felt full. I also gave her permission to call me at any time to scream at me for making her give up her beloved caffeine/soda habit.

Kathy asked, why the diet soda, since it had "only one calorie"? She admitted that she thought I would tell her to give up sweets, or potatoes, or bread, but not something that contained little or no calories. I explained that I felt the most damaging imbalance in her body was her constant intake of diet soda. I also thought that the carbonated ingredients in diet soda could be causing some of her abdominal problems, while serving as a poor substitute for the benefits of pure water. Her body was constantly feeling an odd combination of being bloated yet unsatisfied.

The other assignment I gave Kathy was to find time for active movement, at least ten minutes three times a week, and even more if possible (Step Three). Kathy said she thought she could find twenty minutes a day, five times a week. She said her preferred activity was walking. I approved, but added that she needed a back-up plan if bad weather intervened. She agreed to find a good aerobics tape to use indoors for rainy days. We made plans to meet one week later.

At our second meeting, Kathy reported serious difficulty giving up her diet soda. She complained of painful headaches, irritability, and cramping. I reiterated how difficult it is to break a caffeine/cola habit. Like Jane, she was stunned at how dependent her body had become on soft drinks.

The good news was that she was drinking more water each day, more than she ever imagined possible. Even though Kathy was physically uncomfortable during her initial week, she had gradually reduced her soda intake and had started her walking regimen, which she found pleasantly calming. Over the next week, I urged Kathy to lower her soda intake to one can every other day.

By our third meeting, one week later, Kathy had weaned herself completely off of diet soda. She also discussed a newfound appreciation for the water she was drinking, saying that it made her body feel healthier, and she was beginning to relish the taste. Like many, including myself, she found water most appealing when it was room temperature. Other clients of mine prefer their water chilled and icy cold. Keeping a full pitcher or container of bottled water in the refrigerator is a good idea. But Kathy had also tried heating a mug of water in the microwave to tea or coffee temperatures, and found that she even liked it that way. Other clients have made their water ritual "special," by drinking it from a tall, distinctive glass with ice, or by adding a twist of lemon or lime.

At our fourth meeting, Kathy reported with relief that she was no longer suffering from withdrawal headaches. She noticed less of a daily craving for the diet sodas, and exuded an energy that had been completely absent in our first three meetings. Her kidneys and bladder were adjusting to the volume of water they were processing, and she wasn't urinating as frequently. I applauded her optimism and desire to continue with Step Two. In addition, we had begun to discuss Step One, and she was to set her sights on three nutritious meals a day, plus, happily, a weekly treat. Her frequent walks were helping shed fat while firming up her lower body. What's more, Kathy recognized that true body changes would happen slowly, and for the first time in her life she was willing to take it one day at a time, in hopes that the changes would be permanent this go-round. Her long-lost faith in her body was beginning to return.

Four months into our work together, Kathy had lost ten solid pounds. Her pants and skirts were fitting more comfortably, and she was amazed at her energy level and spunk. She also decided to start jogging one day a week in addition to her walks. I noticed that she always had her bottle of water nearby during our meetings, and that she would drink it throughout our time together. I asked her about her diet soda cravings. She said she did not miss the taste at all and that even though we had agreed she could treat herself with a soda at the movies, she actually preferred water with her popcorn.

I asked how things were going at home. Tears welled up in her eyes and I was afraid for the worst. Instead, she said that becoming a healthier woman had perhaps saved her marriage. She said that recently her husband had complimented her new body, and was excited about the notion of jogging together and sharing healthy habits. He also sheepishly mentioned that her breath had changed, and confessed that when she drank diet sodas all day, he had been turned off by her bad breath. Now that the constant chemical aftertaste was gone, he enjoyed kissing her again.

When we spoke about her feelings of body hatred, she admitted that they were better, but that she still took her clothes off in the dark and felt humiliated by the notion of seeing herself nude—not to mention anyone else seeing her nude. Thus, her naked assignment was to take her clothes off one night a week with all the lights on and look at herself in the mirror and repeat, "I am a strong, beautiful woman with good intentions." She squirmed and wondered if she absolutely had to do that to become healthier. I explained that it was a huge part of accepting herself and loving the healthy body that she was blessed with. To integrate her water "therapy" I told her to then draw a warm bath, immerse herself in it, and imagine herself, naked, floating in a crystal clear tropical pool; allowing the healing water to flow over and through her body, nurturing, cleansing, and replenishing her.

It is now two years later. Kathy has lost twenty pounds. She jogs twice a week, once with her husband and once with Judy. She continues to walk for at least twenty minutes, three times a week, and she drinks eight glasses (sixty-four ounces) of water a day. Kathy is a comfortable size twelve and has decided that her new goal is to lose ten more pounds, not thirty. She undresses every night with the lights on and even allows her husband to watch sometimes. Kathy feels that her marriage has never been healthier or sexier.

The most profound difference that I notice in Kathy is her newfound self-acceptance. She can admit that her prior efforts to change her body were for the wrong reasons: to attain a body she was never meant to have.

I couldn't be more proud of her decision to set her new weight-loss goal at ten pounds instead of thirty. When I first met Kathy, she seemed desperate to physically become someone she was not genetically meant to be. Now, I feel she has come into her own beauty and power and accepts her physical realities, while striving to reach goals that are possible for her.

Even more amazing is that these wonderful changes all began with her commitment to drink lots of water instead of diet soda. That was her remarkable first step. Cheers!

Summary:

Kathy's body was inactive, water deprived, and caffeine dependent due to her diet soda habit. Consequently, she found herself battling weight gain and uncomfortable physical symptoms. She had lost complete faith in herself. By trading diet sodas for water she eventually felt internally cleansed and nourished, and by becoming more active, she saw external changes as well. Today, Kathy is setting a wonderful example for her daughters, while rekindling the excitement and sexuality that had initially brought her and her husband together.

In Step Two, you discover one of the most underpromoted secrets of healthful living and weight loss: drinking enough water. This unheralded "miracle product" offers our bodies so many benefits. If it were a finite commodity, it would make millions for its manufacturers! Yet because it is so available, we take its amazing qualities for granted. Not drinking enough water can actually lead to fluid retention and weight gain. Consuming eight to ten eight-ounce glasses of water each day promotes weight loss, appetite reduction, stomach flattening, younger-looking skin, improved sleep, fewer head and body aches, better muscle function, added energy, and money saved. It's so easy—why not pour yourself a cool glass right now? You'll be on your way to feeling good naked.

STEP 3

WATCH 10 MINUTES OF EXERCISE A DAY CHANGE YOUR FACE AND YOUR LIFE.

Fear Is a Four-Letter Word

Before we talk about how exercise affects the way our faces look, let's talk about some of the fears we have surrounding our appearance. And they are legion. Fear of gaining weight, of losing hair, of wrinkles, of not being as attractive as she is, or as we used to be or, God forbid, fear of . . . being seen naked. Even by ourselves. Silly, right? But stop and think: How did you feel when you saw the word "naked" on the cover of this book? Shocked? Embarrassed? A little naughty? Did you look around before you picked it up, afraid of getting caught? Or did you let out a wild whoop and flip through the pages with abandon? Probably somewhere in between. But I firmly believe that if you were brave enough to pick up a book with the word "naked" in the title—whether you purchased it or are standing in a bookstore reading it right now—you are well on your way to liberating your body.

In truth, most of our fears about our appearances are either unfounded or concern things that are out of our control anyway. So instead of letting our fears paralyze us, or cause us to jump into impulsive, desperate behavior, let's focus instead on the things we can control as we move toward liberating our bodies. As you start to open your mind to new possibilities, you may be surprised how quickly old fears—and old body issues—begin to melt away.

Diets Are about Deprivation. Movement Is about Liberation.

In the first chapter, we talked about the damage that deprivation can do to our bodies and our psyches. Dieting is all about deprivation, and deprivation is not a long-term solution to what ails an overweight or under-appreciated body. Yet when we think about taking action to become the people we want to be, why is it that dieting is the first—and often only—course of action we consider?

I have good news: there are other avenues for improving your body image besides the deprivation of diets. One of the most important is the simple concept of movement.

Now, before that fear of the "e" word (exercise) rears its ugly head, let me explain that the *Feel Good Naked* concept of movement has little to do with fancy health clubs, the latest in spandex fashions, or two-hour workout sessions. I am talking about movement in its most basic form—something anyone with any degree of mobility can do, regardless of physical conditioning, in as little as ten minutes a day. It is about release and liberation, both physically and mentally.

Later in this chapter you will meet my client Jennifer. She is an example of an overachiever who, before we began our work together, suffered through a debilitating eating disorder. As with Erin, I helped Jennifer neutralize her stress by not dieting. In addition, for Jennifer, committing to a simple ten-minute cardiovascular activity each day was medicine for managing her fears and freeing her anxiety. It can work for you, too.

Don't Let Time Be a Bully. Ten Minutes Is Enough.

Why is it that we spend most of our lives making decisions for our bodies without including them in the decision-making process? When we make the mind/body connection, we suddenly realize that our bodies have been screaming at us for years, we just had the volume turned down. Listen up. Our bodies want to move around. They want to be used, they want to sweat profusely. They don't even mind being sore after a fulfilling bout of intense physical labor. If you've ever worked hard in the garden, or moved into a new apartment in one day, or cleaned your whole house because your mother-in-law was on her way over, you know how good utter physical exhaustion can feel. And here's the best part: you can feel that way after just ten minutes.

Don't be afraid it's not enough time. Don't be afraid something else won't get done. If you have time to make coffee or watch the news, you have time to move your body aerobically for ten minutes. The goal is to activate your muscles, to wake up your body. As your muscles are energized and your body temperature elevates, you will feel your heart beating faster. These ten-minute sessions will put the color back in your cheeks. My favorite nonstop ten-minute workouts are:

- Dancing vigorously to upbeat music. I discovered this great release when I first visited Studio 54, a renowned discotheque in New York City. The energy and music immediately made my body pulse with aerobic dance moves. Within ten minutes, I was not only sweating from head to toe, but was in a great mood.

- Cleaning one or two rooms of my apartment. I am an obsessive cleaner and like the challenge of attempting to get two rooms squeaky clean within ten minutes. I aerobically scrub my bathrooms, getting on hands and knees and engaging every muscle in my body. This activity works up quite a sweat and makes taking a shower afterwards a dual reward.

- Walking around the block as many times as possible (don't forget to swing your arms). This is a satisfying workout that I learned when I had exactly ten minutes to get to the bank, before it closed, to make my studio's daily deposit. I always returned to work feeling revived and stretched out.

- Jumping rope continuously. I tried this after becoming infatuated with Sylvester Stallone in the first Rocky movie. Not only was it extremely challenging aerobically, I could swear it reduced the cellulite on the backs of my thighs.

- Walking up and down stairs as fast as possible (take two at a time on the way up). This one I learned while living in a five-story walk-up in New York City. My butt never looked better than when I lived there. If I was unable to exercise on any given day, I would repeatedly walk up and down these five flights before turning in for the night. Within three minutes, I would be perspiring. After ten minutes, I was dripping with sweat, feeling muscles in my buttocks I didn't even know existed.

- Mowing the lawn with a push mower. I had never mowed a lawn in my life until I visited friends in Connecticut and was trying to come up with a way to thank them for their hospitality. The grass obviously needed cutting, I spotted an old lawn mower in the garage, and the rest is history. This dreaded task offers a wonderful opportunity to walk continuously while pushing the weight of a mower, which provides an additional isometric arm exercise.

- Parking ten minutes away from the grocery store and buying heavy stuff. I love to do this. In fact, I will deliberately park ten minutes away on days that I buy bottled water, laundry detergent, and orange juice. Carrying loaded bags gives my arms a wonderful pump of adrenaline. It is also a good chance to work on my posture and abdominal and back strength.

- Washing the car (yes, this is something you can do yourself). I like washing my bright red Volkswagen Beetle as quickly as I can while trying to use as many muscles as possible. I put motivating music in the tape player and go for it. If you cannot wash your entire car in ten minutes, try vacuuming the inside within ten minutes while contracting your abdominal muscles at the same time.

- Making love. What I will say about this one is that you no longer need to feel embarrassed if you sweat like an athlete while making love. Think of lovemaking as a wonderful opportunity to burn extra calories while releasing all kinds of powerful endorphins. While you might want to spend more than ten minutes on this workout, if you give it your best energy, you'll not only burn calories within ten minutes, but also receive the undying gratitude of your lover. Again, a dual reward.

Now, please understand, the ten-minute approach to exercise is for people who are basically healthy, but currently doing little or nothing aerobically because they think anything less than a sixty-minute workout is not worth the effort. Ten minutes daily is the minimum for infusing a healthy dose of physical activity into your life. It is not appropriate for those who have a significant amount of weight to lose, who may need more activity (see Susan, Step Four). And it is not for those who have medical conditions that prevent them from exercising at all. Check with your doctor before beginning any regular exercise program.

But by all means, do begin. Start slowly and give it a chance. Enjoy your favorite ten-minute workouts at least four times a week for three weeks—preferably more often. At the end of three weeks, notice how you feel sexier, happier, and more comfortable in your skin. If you like what these sessions are doing for you, then by all means keep going. I urge you to try and commit to at least ten minutes of movement every day, or twenty minutes four times a week. Longer if you like, and if you have the time. Think of these ten-minute sessions as a good chat with your very best friend in the whole wide world, one you get to have every day if you wish. Lucky you.

About the Face

Fear shows up first on our face; we hold our mouths tightly, we lower our heads, narrow our eyes—we withdraw. A fearful face appears tense. But a body that has put fear on hold and moved around for ten minutes a day supports a more open and beautiful face. What happens physically during exercise is that your busy heart sends more blood everywhere, including your face, causing you to become slightly flushed with color. Exercising also makes you perspire, which is an effective way to reduce swelling in your face, if, like me, you tend to hold water weight in the facial area. Mentally, you feel stronger and more confident after exercising; you're more relaxed and less bothered by . . . stuff. The overall effect after these ten-minute sessions is a prettier, happier, more youthful face.

When I see photographs of myself, I can always tell by my facial expression if I exercised that day or not. I can also tell when I look at my face in the mirror. Before exercising, I tend to be hyper-critical, noticing my deep forehead lines, crow's-feet and drooping eyelids. After exercising, I tend to admire my glowing cheeks, soulful eyes, and full lips. As you will see with Jennifer, her personal photographs also taught her a great deal about how we perceive ourselves—and how we want others to see us.

Jennifer's Story

Jennifer's tale is common to many women. She struggles to feel good about herself and is convinced that she must be a grave disappointment in the eyes of her very successful mother.

Jennifer is almost six feet tall.
Her mother is just slightly over five feet tall.

Jennifer's mother is an impressive feminist who has helped break the barriers encountered by many women of her generation. As for Jennifer, I have rarely met a more dynamic woman: attractive, accomplished, and with an uncanny ability to listen and respond to people as if she has known them all her life. She is highly educated and financially secure and is constantly pushing herself beyond her limits. Jennifer is the quintessential overachiever. But despite her accomplishments, Jennifer did not feel at home in her body, she did not feel good naked.

Jennifer came to me during an election campaign in which she was working hard to rally New York City's female voters. Like most campaign volunteers, she was supremely dedicated and determined not to stop until the last vote was counted. Jennifer was referred to me by her sister-in-law, a devoted client of mine, and she began by participating in my group classes, giving, in true Jennifer fashion, nothing less than 100 percent. I immediately noticed her strong, beautiful body and was quite surprised when she asked if we could work together privately. This was a woman who, despite her impressive determination and control, seemed inclined to hide her statuesque body behind a cloak of humility. My curiosity was piqued. We agreed to start our private sessions after the campaign ended.

During our first session, I complimented Jennifer on her performance in class, as well as her magnificent body. She was visibly shocked at my observations, incredulous that I found her body not only acceptable, but outstanding. Jennifer only saw how fat she'd become during the grueling campaign. She was disgusted. She told me she hated her body.

It disturbed me to realize that Jennifer saw herself as fat. Jennifer is not fat. Her problem was far more serious: Jennifer felt fat. I was determined to get to the bottom of her fat mind-set and set her free with new ways of thinking and moving. I asked Jennifer to bring me a photograph of herself that she thought best represented the way she looked, so I could discern what she thought she looked like. She picked a picture that showed her body from the waist up. I asked about her lower body and she moaned and said, "I would never pick a photograph of myself that shows my lower body. I'm too disgusted with my huge legs." I told her that before bed each night, I wanted her to look at herself naked in front of a full-length mirror and repeat three times slowly, "My legs are healthy, strong, and beautiful." She was also to repeat the same practice first thing in the morning before showering. Reluctantly, she agreed to this naked ritual.

As our work progressed, Jennifer shared with me her paralyzing fear of being seen as a failure by her mother. For the record, Jennifer had been offered a full scholarship to law school, had created an organization that raised grant money for the education of underprivileged children, and was helping care for her ailing father. Clearly this was a very special woman . . . and one who could not seem to appreciate her own value or slow down. She was also a woman who was deeply afraid to acknowledge the differences between herself and her mother.

One of the first things I uncovered about Jennifer was that when her life got crazy, she stopped exercising altogether. Common, but especially detrimental for her, since it allowed many fears and negative thoughts to surface. She thought that if she couldn't spend an hour engaged in a serious workout, five times a week, why bother? I encouraged Jennifer to release her fear through simple cardiovascular activity, even if it was just for ten minutes a day. I told her she didn't need to change clothes, she didn't need to go to a club, she didn't even need bulky exercise equipment—she could get her exercise in any variety of simple activities, such as walking, jumping rope, dancing aerobically, or just following a fitness tape. She agreed that she would do some kind of movement for ten minutes each day—even if it was just climbing the stairs to her apartment.

These short bursts of activity had a quick and positive effect on Jennifer. Clarity and honesty began to surface, and several weeks into our sessions, Jennifer confessed to a problem with bulimia (eating a large quantity of food, then purging it from the body by vomiting) that had dominated her life since her late teens.

Affecting an estimated seven million women in the United States, eating disorders are distressingly common, and often complicated. Control issues tend to be at the center of most eating disorders. Generally speaking, women who suffer from bulimia are often raised in a chaotic family setting where they receive mixed messages about food and weight. Those who suffer from anorexia are generally raised in a rigid and controlling family where nothing but the best is tolerated. But eating disorders can affect anyone, of any background or family history.

According to the Anorexia Nervosa and Bulimia Association, a number of other personal factors can contribute to the development of eating disorders such as bulimia. Those factors include:

- Low self-esteem
- Feelings of ineffectiveness/perfectionism
- Feelings of being powerless and being controlled by outside forces or people
- Fear of maturation (common among adolescents)
- Societal and media pressures to have an ultra-slim body

They also note that self-induced vomiting can lead to a wide scope of ills, including:

- Hypokalemia (low levels of potassium), which is characterized by fatigue, muscle weakness, muscle spasms, irritability, and depression
- Gastrointestinal problems such as bloating, constipation, and inflammation of and damage to the esophagus
- Nutritional deficiencies due to poor absorption of protein, carbohydrates, and fats as well as lipids
- Dental problems such as loss of enamel and numerous cavities

In keeping with these findings, Jennifer exhibited several of the most typical causal factors, including low self-esteem, the need for perfection, and the feeling that even though she was thirty-two years old, she continued to be greatly influenced and controlled by her mother. Personally, I have noticed that clients with eating disorders are often women who have never felt totally accepted or loved by their mothers.

Jennifer also felt physically vulnerable when comparing her looks to the standards of "beauty" that are constantly bombarding us through the media. Ironically, however, Jennifer acknowledged that her eating disorder did little to relieve her feelings of inadequacy; instead it made her feel worse. Happiness seemed to have been vacuumed from her life.

Jennifer felt an incredible amount of shame around the fact that she was so accomplished and capable in so many areas of her life, and so out-of-control in her dealings with food. Yet not surprisingly, this scenario reflected an eerily similar pattern to her mother's lifestyle. It was interesting to hear that for all of her professional acclaim, her mother never ate three meals in one day. When Jennifer was a growing, six-foot-tall teenager, her mother had repeatedly drummed into her head that eating three meals a day would make her fat. As a result, Jennifer would become voraciously hungry, eating as many as five meals each day, although any food that exceeded two meals a day was purged through vomiting. Regardless of how these issues arose, the fact was that Jennifer had serious and potentially life-threatening body-image problems.

When Jennifer revealed her sad secret to me, I encouraged her to seek the help of a professional therapist who specialized in eating disorders, and to consider attending Overeaters Anonymous (O.A.) meetings. Designed as a twelve-step program much like Alcoholics Anonymous, Overeaters Anonymous has been a lifeline of sanity and support for many of my clients. Here, people with eating disorders can gather in anonymity to share their experience, strength, and hope.

It was a huge step for Jennifer to confront her eating disorder and her fear of getting fat, but she did. She sought the help of a skilled therapist in overcoming her tendency to lapse into bulimia during stressful times. She began attending O.A. meetings—awkwardly at first, but slowly Jennifer was able to accept the healing comfort of others who shared her anxieties and problems.

And for at least ten minutes each day, Jennifer calmed down through cardio-vascular activity. As her schedule allowed, she increased her "movement" sessions to more than ten minutes, but even when she was most frantic, she never abandoned her promise to find ten minutes a day for aerobic activity.

Even this short duration of movement was enough to keep her mind and body in balance regarding what, and how, she ate. It also helped her feel more positive about herself.

Eventually, Jennifer stopped seeing food as her enemy, gradually replacing her negative associations with the simple joy of eating three meals and two mini-meals each day. Once she began eating the proper amount of food (Steps One and Five), she stopped bingeing and vomiting.

For Jennifer, the best reward—and surprise—was that eating well did not cause her to gain weight. Her commitment to frequent cardiovascular movements—even in busy times—combined with her newfound ability to digest an appropriate daily intake of food (including three meals and two mini-meals) helped her body find a comfortable balance. Just as important were her weekly therapy sessions, where she continued to process her psychological issues.

By combining therapy with the *Feel Good Naked* lifestyle, Jennifer slowly began to perceive herself as a beautiful, well-proportioned woman with great bone structure and height. Once she could admit and accept that she was not a fat woman, she began sleeping better, carrying herself more confidently, and making sound decisions based on her own values and ambitions, not those of her mother. In turn, while her mother remained critical, Jennifer began to receive positive affirmations from other people, both in terms of her body and her optimistic outlook on life.

I tried to help Jennifer understand that while approval might never be forthcoming from her mother, it was Jennifer's responsibility to give it to herself. In each of our sessions, I would repeat over and over "do it for yourself, not for your mother." Once Jennifer accepted her disappointment in the woman who had had so much influence on her life, she was able to have a healthier, more honest relationship with herself and with her mother.

She eventually confronted her mom, telling her that she was through with feeling guilty about food and that she needed to eat at least three meals a day to support her busy schedule. Her mother responded with a comment about how wonderful Jennifer had been looking and how thin she had become. Jennifer told her mother that she in fact was not thinner, but that she was healthier and more balanced. Her mother looked confused. Jennifer finally accepted that her mother would never "get it," and no one could change that reality. For the first time in her life, Jennifer vowed to not allow her mother's opinions or expectations change her or make her feel like a loser.

I find it fascinating that it was only when Jennifer began treating her body with love and respect, instead of abusing it in the name of seeking outside approval, that she began receiving the approval she'd been craving for so long. It is a self-fulfilling prophecy: our own opinion of ourselves influences others' opinions of us much more than we realize.

Jennifer now lives in Washington, D.C. She continues to eat wisely and joyfully, and to put aside her anxieties for at least ten minutes a day by engaging in a cardiovascular activity. When her schedule permits, she will gladly exercise longer, but when all she has is ten minutes, she dances to loud, invigorating music alone in her apartment, jumps rope on the roof of her building, walks around her neighborhood as fast as she can, or walks up and down the twelve flights of stairs in her building. She also finds that committing to her ten-minute routine before seeing her mother gives her a healthier approach to her mom's potential jabs and negativity.

I recently received a full-body photograph of Jennifer that actually showcased her legs. She looked marvelous. I was curious to see how my new photograph of Jennifer would compare with the original picture she had given to me, and was amazed at what I saw. Here was the same tall, beautiful woman I had met three years ago, but her face looked years younger. Her eyes sparkled and she was smiling with deep contentment. Jennifer accepts that she will never be waif-thin, and she no longer wants to be. She knows firsthand that lasting beauty comes from the inside. When I turned the photograph over, she had written on the back, "My legs are healthy, strong, and beautiful."

During the difficult periods of our work together, Jennifer and I referred often to the words of an Eastern philosopher, words she now keeps taped to her bathroom mirror: "Be grateful for the weeds you have in your mind, because eventually they will enrich your practice."

Summary:

In addition to her negative self-image, Jennifer also had a serious eating disorder, a chronic problem that is unfortunately shared by millions of women. Jennifer's issues were primarily about fear and anxiety: fear of not being good enough, fear of getting fat, fear of losing control, anxiety over not being as successful as her mother. Her first step toward happiness was to give herself permission to ignore her fears for ten minutes a day while engaging in cardiovascular movement.

The remarkable power of a ten-minute cardiovascular activity not only diminished her anxieties, it also allowed Jennifer to let go of her unrealistic and damaging ideas about how her body should look. Today Jennifer accepts that she is a strong, healthy woman. She eats three balanced meals a day, plus two nutritious mini-meals, and she hasn't vomited after a meal in eight years. Once Jennifer experienced the positive impact that the third *Feel Good Naked* step had on her entire life, she began practicing the other nine steps, one at a time. She believes that incorporating the *Feel Good Naked* program into her daily life is the most gratifying choice she has ever made.

Whether your issues are the same as Jennifer's or completely different, try Step Three. Spend ten minutes a day doing aerobic exercise. Your heart and lungs will become more powerful, your circulation will improve, your face will glow and relax. A face that is glowing and relaxed is a pretty face. There's not one woman on the planet who isn't happier and more attractive after ten minutes of cardiovascular activity a day.

STEP 4

SCHEDULE FITNESS APPOINTMENTS IN WRITING EACH WEEK.

Denial Is Hazardous to Your Health

In Step Three, we discussed the importance of moving aerobically for at least ten minutes a day or twenty minutes four times a week. "Ten minutes?" you may have asked yourself. "Hey, even I can find ten minutes a day. This will be a snap." Perhaps. But if you're like 99 percent of the women I work with, finding those ten minutes once your day is in full gear is about as likely as finding all of your children's lost socks. You say you will do it, but trust me, you won't—unless you make a concerted effort to write down your fitness appointments.

Let's face it, everything is fast and furious in this maniacal new century, whether it's shoveling a meal down in seconds, talking on the phone while checking your e-mail, or driving and applying makeup at the same time. It's no wonder we are all deeply exhausted and stressed out. How can you possibly find time to exercise when you cannot even find time to call back a good friend who left you a voice mail a week ago?

Now add the reality of relationships and children into this frenzied formula . . . yikes . . . exercise is most definitely going to be what gets pushed aside. Ironically, exercise might just be the one thing that can offer you relief. I cannot believe how often people say to me, "I would love to exercise, but I can't—I have absolutely no time for it." Yet my clients who have survived heart attacks or cancer seem to find the time to exercise. What is the difference? They have accepted that exercising their bodies is a matter of life or death. Why wait until that point? Instead, acknowledge the importance of this physical appointment with yourself today, and realize that the only way to honor this priority is to schedule it in writing each week.

I cannot stress the importance of this step enough. It is amazing how successfully my clients respond to a scheduled fitness appointment as opposed to a mental commitment. If you think you'll exercise without writing it down, you either don't need this book—or you're in serious denial. There are simply too many other priorities that will pull you away when it's not written down. And if you're creative about what you choose to do for your aerobic activity (refer back to my favorite non-exercise workouts in Step Three), your fitness sessions don't have to be boring and monotonous. They just have to be written down.

Later in this chapter you will meet Susan. Susan had no idea how she went from 150 to 350 pounds. All she knew when we began working together was that she was busy, preoccupied, and overwhelmed. She kept a daily planner that was always full—with everything except what was most important.

In Today's World, Sex Isn't the Only Thing That Needs to Be Scheduled

When I was fat, I can remember thinking in bed at night that I wanted to take a walk or jog the next day, yet I would never quite get around to it. Every jog that I attempted made me feel better, yet I would still allow a month to elapse between these cardiovascular outings. It's that odd feeling of knowing you would really like to exercise, but all of a sudden you find yourself reading the paper instead. Or paying bills. Or watering the plants. Or any one of the many things that could and should get done, in a perfect world.

I first learned the essential nature of scheduling exercise in boarding school. I credit my roommate Hamer for teaching me how to do this. She was the one who would make me commit to a specific time, before bed, to jog the next day. I began to notice that if we did not make this verbal commitment the night before, we never made time the next day. Scheduling exercise dates is a wonderful notion for people who need others to depend on them in order to show up. One of my clients found a neighbor to walk with every morning at 6:00 A.M. She confessed to me that the only reason she would wake up every morning to walk was to show up for her neighbor. She feared that without this shared ritual, she would opt to sleep instead of walk. So, in the beginning of your *Feel Good Naked* process, find a neighbor or friend to agree to meet you at a specific, scheduled time each week. It works.

When I started college, I had a new roommate who was inactive. Eventually this forced me to become self-motivated, but initially this was not easy for me. It was not until I gained the "freshman ten" that I realized I must schedule my own fitness appointments. I found it difficult to jog alone since I had become accustomed to sharing this ritual with Hamer. Instead, I decided to try Shackelfords exercise studio, a place where I could take classes with others. It did not take long for me to become committed to these group classes.

I could not believe how great I felt after each workout. I designed my weekly schedule to include at least five exercise classes each week at Shackelfords. During my sophomore year I became an employee of Shackelfords while carrying a full class load. I soon learned that if I didn't write down my weekly exercise appointments along with my college classes and work hours, I would not make the time to take care of myself. I also learned the necessity of juggling multiple tasks in order to stay in top physical form. My goals were becoming clearer as I consciously scheduled each week of my life. The accomplishment of fulfilling many responsibilities, including my responsibility to myself to stay healthy, would become the experience that most prepared me for life after college.

Upon graduation, I moved to New York City, which proved to be one big scheduling challenge—whether it was planning pleasure around work or work around errands or errands around eating or eating around sleeping. New York runs at such an exhausting pace that the only way to survive is to be organized, scheduled, and fast. Running an exercise studio meant that I also needed to schedule the exercise classes that were offered from 7 A.M. until 10 P.M. each day of the week.

I began to notice that the women with the most impressive bodies were the clients who showed up every day at the same time, without fail. I can remember the actress Stockard Channing was one of those examples. She would take the 5:30 P.M. class every day and then run to Lincoln Center to appear in an 8 P.M. performance. I was always impressed with her figure and focus. Obviously there were millions of other things she could have done instead of taking an exercise class. However, she scheduled it, showed up, and benefited as a result. Her daily commitment reminded me of my own experience in college—it was only when I enrolled in an exercise class that I was able to make it a priority.

It Must Be Important—It's in Writing

Over the years, I saw that this scheduled consistency was such an obvious key to physical success, I began to require that all of my private clients write down, in pen, their fitness appointments each week. I remember my client Betty, a lawyer, who would open her appointment book and hand it to me to prove there were no openings for fitness appointments. I would always find a space in her book for exercise, even if it meant waking up at 5 A.M. She would shoot me a disgusted look and reluctantly agree to meet me in

Central Park at 5:30 A.M., while angrily writing it down in her appointment book. And, without fail, at 6:30 A.M. after our workout was complete, Betty would be glowing, happy, and ready for all of her daily demands.

There is just something official about seeing plans written down in ink. It makes them much harder to dismiss. Pam, another client, wrote down her fitness appointments for a full four weeks before ever actually engaging in any physical activity. Her plan was to appease me by writing them down, and then to ignore them. But her plan backfired. The accumulated guilt of seeing her missed appointments every time she opened her daily organizer affected her. Pam reluctantly admitted that having her failed commitments staring back at her in black and white gave her the necessary kick start to begin exercising.

Schedule your fitness appointments on Sunday for the following Monday through Sunday. Do not wait until Monday to write down your appointments, or you will again find an excuse or feel too busy, since the week is already in full swing. You would not call your boss on Monday to schedule a meeting that same day. You would call several days before. Fitness appointments are just as important as a meeting with your boss. Schedule them in advance.

Write your appointments down wherever you will see them most often, whether it's in a daily planner you carry in your purse, a table-size calendar on your desk at work, or the family calendar at home. Don't think that a ten-minute exercise appointment is not important enough to have a written space in your day's plans. Think about it: you write down doctor appointments, hair appointments, even appointments with the window cleaners. Surely a date with yourself is as important as one with the window cleaners.

As much as I believed and professed the power of this scheduling ritual, it wasn't until I began working with Susan that I appreciated the absolute necessity of this fourth *Feel Good Naked* step.

Susan's Story

Susan and I first met at an anniversary party of mutual friends. The moment we spoke, I was blown away by her personal power. Susan is a large woman with an electric presence, someone who lights up any room. I was intrigued to learn that she worked for the Girl Scouts of America. As we talked about her job, I found myself thinking what a perfect career for someone who was the embodiment of "girl power." It was easy to envision Susan working in an atmosphere that promotes the slogan "Where girls grow strong." Susan seemed to be the ultimate example of an empowered female.

Susan and I continued to see each other socially over the next year. Although she was in her thirties and single, she never seemed to dwell on the negative aspects of being alone. Instead, Susan always surrounded herself with friends. Because Susan seemed socially comfortable, I assumed she accepted her large frame and felt good naked. Therefore, I was surprised when she asked me if we could schedule a fitness therapy session.

During our first session, I realized how wrong my initial impressions had been (contrary to my experience with Erin in Step One). Susan confided in me that she felt like a healthy person trapped in a 350-pound body. When I asked her how she believed she had climbed to that weight, she honestly had no idea. This is surprisingly common with very overweight people. It's as if a switch gets turned off after 200 pounds. Denial and sadness typically set in and food becomes a secret companion in the dark night. As my work progressed with Susan, I learned that her weight was in fact a shield. It allowed her a subconscious hiding space from all things that she believed could potentially hurt her: intimate relationships, work promotions, new friendships, traveling opportunities, etc. It wasn't until we had worked together for six months that she broke down in hysterical tears with the realization that her weight was the greatest hurt of all, and that food was her only real comfort, friend, pleasure, and reward. For all the flocks of people always buzzing around Susan, she felt close to few of them. For all of her power and charisma, Susan felt little contentment inside.

At our first meeting, I explained to Susan that she needed to do only two things for the time being: schedule her fitness appointments in writing each week, and show up for these appointments. She looked at me with surprise and confusion and wondered if that was really all she had to do. I explained that for now, that was it. However, I also explained that her movement sessions needed to be more than the ten-minute minimum. Since her goal was to shed a significant amount of weight, she needed to engage in enough cardiovascular activity to increase her metabolism, and burn the stored fat her body had accumulated.

As I mentioned in Step Three, ten minutes a day is the minimum to get the cobwebs out and achieve a healthy balance of activity in your life. It is not intended as a route to major weight loss. If you are trying to lose more than ten pounds, you will have to boost the amount of time you spend moving aerobically, working up to at least thirty minutes, four or five times a week.

In Bob Greene and Oprah Winfrey's book, *Make the Connection*, Bob shares that while Oprah is blessed with many gifts, a favorable metabolism is not one of them. He explains that unfortunately, because of her slow metabolism, she must work much harder and longer than most people to attain a desirable weight. In this way, Susan was similar to Oprah.

I asked Susan to talk to her doctor about what would be a safe, beneficial cardiovascular activity for her, and to have him recommend a safe duration of time for this outing. With his blessings, Susan decided that she could commit to an hour-long walk, six days a week.

Susan wondered why she needed to write down her appointments if it was just a walking excursion. I explained that if she didn't write it down, she wouldn't do it. She then tried again to avoid the written part by telling me that she would just take a daily walk, no big deal. I explained that it is a very big deal, and that unless she treated these walking appointments like business meetings or doctor appointments, she would find it much too tempting to fill her walking time with other things. She finally agreed, and promised to e-mail me her weekly schedules every Monday morning, having written them down the Sunday night before.

Several things happened for Susan during her first week of walking. She realized her feet were killing her and that she would need to invest in a new pair of walking shoes. She realized it had been a very long time since she had walked for a full hour and that she was exhausted. At the same time, she couldn't believe how much better she felt at the end of her walk compared to when she began. And, she felt wonderfully encouraged that she was physically up to the task. Yet, the most powerful realization of all was Susan's acknowledgment that she had been in denial about her weight for years. Writing down her appointments forced her to come face-to-face with her crippling denial. It took only one week of scheduling these walking appointments for Susan to realize that she could not remain in denial if she was writing down her exercise appointments. In other words, scheduling exercise to combat her weight gain forced Susan to come to terms with her size.

As the weeks progressed, Susan found that her best time for a fitness appointment was in the early morning before her day began. This is true for many of my clients. Early morning fitness appointments are especially helpful for people who are beginning a fitness routine for the first time or trying to start a routine after giving it up for a long period of time. It is also the best time for mothers to schedule exercise since the demands of motherhood increase when children wake up. The fact is: if you exercise first thing in the morning, you have a greater chance of showing up for your fitness appointments. It's also a remarkable jump start for the rest of your day. Bob Greene even mentions that exercising first thing in the morning helps your metabolism stay elevated throughout the day—which burns calories even when you're not exercising.

For Susan, these written appointments became the first tangible measure of a successful fitness commitment—the first real fitness accomplishment she had ever achieved. With that incentive, she began the trauma of embracing her 350-pound body, which was already beginning to change. As each week progressed and I would receive Susan's Monday morning e-mail reporting her fitness appointments for the week, I began to wonder how her emotional state was reacting to her body's new physical commitment. We agreed to meet once a week and take her hour-long walk together. These walks became fascinating and gut-wrenching as Susan opened up to me all of the heartbreaks of being a fat woman in our society. She purged her disgust, her embarrassment, her body hatred, and her desire to finally do something about it.

While we both could see heartening changes in Susan's body, she was frustrated that the immediate results were not more dramatic. She felt that if she was willing to write these six appointments down each week and show up for them that she should be a size fourteen already. Susan had spent thirty-two years being rewarded for her take-charge approach to every other aspect of her life, and now, with two months of effort under her belt, she wanted immediate results. Over and over I would explain, fast results mean temporary change, slow results mean legitimate life changes.

As her anger built around the slow pace of change, I realized it was really deep-seated anger about being fat. So I asked Susan to describe what it felt like to be 350 pounds. She would practically scream out, "It feels like I'll never know the sensation of being kissed. I'll never be able to attend a movie without overhearing people's whispers about me breaking the chair. I'll never be able to board a plane without the terror that I can't fit in the seat. I'll never know what it feels like to shop in normal clothing stores. I'll never walk into a restaurant without kids pointing at me and laughing. I'll never be considered smart since fat people are assumed to be stupid. I'll never know the experience of true happiness." I would encourage these outbursts, knowing how valuable it is to release the feelings instead of eating them in the form of junk food.

In honor of Susan's six-month anniversary with her fitness program, I assigned her the task of taking off her clothes in private and sitting naked for five minutes. As silly or embarrassing as it may seem, this ritual allows a person to begin the process of accepting her body from the inside out. To know yourself, and your body, to understand your strengths and weaknesses, fears and joys, and what you dislike or like about yourself, is the greatest opportunity you have to make the necessary changes to be a happier person. I explained to Susan that these five minutes would probably feel like an eternity and that during this time, I wanted her to figure out what her favorite parts of her body were, as well as her least favorite.

The next day when we met to walk, she confided in me that she had felt utterly terrified being naked, but that she was thrilled at having accomplished the task. Her least favorite body parts were her thighs and her upper arms and her favorites were her eyes and her ankles. I agreed that her eyes and ankles deserved first place. And, that I wanted her to continue this naked ritual once a week.

Our walking sessions sometimes led to both of us crying, yet at the end of the hour, we always reached hopeful conclusions. I continually repeated to Susan that if it took her thirty-two years to become a 350-pound woman, she would need to allow more than a few months to shed her excess weight. I also reminded her that the only way to lose weight successfully is through a commitment to exercise and conscious eating.

As I had expected, at various points in her life, Susan had tried every diet known to man. She remembered her first diet attempt at 200 pounds. At 350 pounds, she couldn't count how many times she had been on a fad diet. Despite the fact that not one of her many diets had produced long-lasting effects, Susan had trouble letting go of the promise of quick weight loss that accompanies fad diets. Often, I reminded her that if the weight comes off quickly, prepare to gain it back quickly. On the other hand, if it comes off slowly, it is more likely to stay off. Real change takes time. There are no secrets, and diets don't work (Step One). In fact, I told Susan that the crash diets she had tried had likely contributed to her weight gain, by teaching her body to need too few calories, thus lowering her body's metabolism.

Recently, I read in *Marilu Henner's Total Health Makeover* that the diet industry is worth more than 30 billion dollars a year with a 95 percent failure rate.

I could tell Susan was torn: eager for the dramatic results dieting promised, but relieved she didn't have to torture herself with food deprivation. I told her she never had to diet again, but that down the road, she would need to learn how to eat with awareness (Step Five). For now, she simply needed to write down her fitness appointments each week and show up for them.

As Susan continued to show up for her fitness appointments and her naked rituals, many wonderful things began to happen, albeit slowly. Within three months, her clothes were fitting more loosely, and her associates at the Girl Scouts began noticing her physical changes. She was elated to find her pulse rate had lowered, her breathing had become more comfortable, and her energy level had increased. By simply writing her fitness appointments down each week and showing up for these appointments, Susan was finally beginning to lose the burden of her weight. By pushing herself to peel away her clothes in order to sit with herself naked for five minutes, she was gaining a newfound self-confidence.

Susan also confided to me that her naked rituals were teaching her a new understanding of how to be alone with herself. She started recognizing the fact that she constantly surrounded herself with people as a means of avoiding being alone. The *Feel Good Naked* philosophy was beginning to build Susan's self-esteem in a way that she had never experienced before.

Today, two years later, Susan has lost more than 100 pounds. She credits this weight loss to her weekly fitness appointments. She would never consider not writing them down, since she knows that this written commitment is what keeps her physically and mentally in check. Susan is a firm believer in the fourth step and has begun embracing the other nine steps as well. She also admitted that she has become relaxed with her nakedness, aware of the freedom it brings her.

Susan's revelation of being comfortable naked reminded me of the one and only time I went to a nude beach. It was in the south of France. The first five naked minutes, I was brutally self-conscious; however, I would have felt even more uncomfortable to be the only one in a bathing suit. After a nap on my lounge chair, I awoke with more confidence to go with the flow, and by the third hour, I was swimming, sunning, walking, and running, completely grateful for the freedom and fun, and aware of how beautiful and natural all of the many naked bodies around me looked. At first I had noticed every bosom and penis. By the end of the day, it could not have mattered less. Try to be naked with yourself for five minutes a week. At the end of six months, don't be surprised to find yourself cooking, cleaning, and talking on the phone in the buff.

What Susan continues to share with me, as do countless clients, is her surprise and amazement that she can reach her physical goals without dieting. Virtually everyone I work with has the belief that genuine change is about drastic deprivation. The moment my clients begin to trust my *Feel Good Naked* ten-step program is the moment when they joyfully accept that honesty, coupled with consciousness, breeds the most impressive changes, not dieting.

While Susan's newfound body consciousness is a profound gift, I also gently remind her to never forget the pain and discomfort of the 350-pound woman who found me. That woman was a remarkably brave person who had the courage and wherewithal to make a life change. To honor that person, she must continue to write down her fitness appointments each week, staying committed to her greatest priority—her body.

Summary:

Susan's issues were about denial: the denial of gaining 200 pounds, of allowing herself to go from 150 to 350 pounds. Despite possessing a charismatic, powerful personality and surrounding herself with others, Susan realized she was using her weight to hide from everything. She was sabotaging her happiness by mindlessly using food as a shield.

Susan had half-heartedly tried many fad diets, and was convinced that dieting was the only way to reverse her weight gain. Her first step toward success was being willing to engage in regular physical activity—and agreeing to write down her fitness appointments each week. By writing down her appointments, she could no longer deny her body size.

Susan also started spending five minutes a week naked. By getting to know her body better, she was able to appreciate her subtle improvements, thanks to her familiarity with every curve and nuance.

Slowly, Susan began to appreciate the lasting progress she was making, and was able to adopt other *Feel Good Naked* steps.

Whether you are heavy or thin, Step Four can be the difference between making fitness a priority in your life—and giving other responsibilities more importance than your own health and well-being. Schedule fitness appointments—even if they're only ten minutes—in writing each week. Do not assume you will do it without this written reminder because you won't. Whether you're meeting a friend for a yoga class or simply taking a walk, write it down.

Remember to use early mornings as your scheduled fitness time if your days are especially busy (whose aren't?) or if your life seems to get more hectic as the day progresses. Your health is as important as your infant's feeding, your teenager's soccer practice, or your client's deadline. It deserves the same priority.

STEP 5

DON'T STOP EATING. STOP EATING IN FRONT OF THE TV.

The Visible Effects of Invisible Eating

Quick. Name everything you've eaten in the past twelve hours. Then describe in graphic detail the distinct tastes and textures of each bite you consumed.

What's that? You're having trouble remembering?

Don't worry, you're not alone. Eating consciously and with purpose is one of the toughest things to achieve with today's pace of life. Yet it is an essential step toward adopting a healthy lifestyle through the *Feel Good Naked* program.

Here is the mantra I want you to repeat:

"I will observe and decide what to eat, then enjoy my choices with awareness."

If you can follow this simple directive, trust me—you will be feeling good naked in no time.

I have had several low points in my life when I ate with blind abandon, in an effort to avoid unpleasant feelings. You should see how fast I can put away a jumbo bag of potato chips—without remembering a single chip. I'm here to tell you, it doesn't work. Mindless, unconscious eating will not—I repeat—will not eliminate painful feelings. In fact, your original angst will be compounded, since in addition to your mental pain, you aren't able to manage your weight effectively either. And the truth is, being emotionally distraught and fat is much harder than taking control of your eating habits, addressing your emotional pitfalls, and making changes.

So much of unbalanced eating is about trying to fill the voids in our hearts. We try to use food as a companion. We eat to not feel—lonely, sad, desperate, depressed, isolated—the list goes on. But by being aware enough to stop yourself before you begin unconscious eating, and defining the troubling feelings you're trying to avoid, you can actually help yourself in two ways: by stopping the unchecked inflow of excess calories, and by confronting your feelings and working to overcome them.

Ask yourself the next time you feel one hand frantically feeding your mouth, while the other hand pushes the television remote, "WHAT DO I FEEL RIGHT THIS SECOND?" These are usually the feelings you are trying to stuff away—or eat away. Unless you address them, those feelings will remain buried under layers of fat.

Dinner for One—Delightful

My client, Sally, had an impressive body when we first met. Her goals were specific and attainable. However, one year into our work together, she suffered a horrible divorce, which left her living alone for the first time in a decade. As a result of her loneliness, Sally used the television as her dinner companion, and quickly gained ten pounds. When we addressed her feelings about eating dinner alone, she began to get in touch with her deep despair and loneliness. Once Sally identified these feelings, and began seeing a therapist, she also began to eat her dinners with a newfound awareness. I suggested she play soothing music during her dinners alone, instead of watching television. Sally's extra weight came off within weeks of eating dinner mindfully.

Like Sally, after I left my first marriage, I had to learn how to eat dinners alone. While we were married, my ex-husband and I had dined out regularly, often in New York's finest restaurants, where I never had trouble eating with awareness. (Later in this chapter, I will share my restaurant secrets with those of you who eat out frequently.)

Once our marriage was over, and I lived alone, I was dumbfounded by the emotional challenges, not the least of which was what to do with myself at dinnertime. It was easy for me to eat healthy foods for breakfast and lunch. Yet the moment it became dark outside, I dreaded the prospect of eating dinner alone in my apartment. I hate leftovers, I hate wasting food, and I didn't know how to shop for one person for dinner. For my first few single weeks, dinner consisted of a bag of pretzels, followed by a pint of Ben and Jerry's® ice cream. I always consumed these "dinners" in front of the television, completely unaware when the pint of ice cream was empty. I began buying two pints a night, since the first pint was generally finished before the second commercial break.

Sally and I were not alone in our zoned-out approach to eating in front of the TV—or in the weight gain we experienced as a result. Over the course of a year, researchers at the University of Minnesota's School of Public Health followed the eating, exercising, and TV-watching habits of more than a thousand men and women who were trying not to gain weight. Surprise: at the end of the year, those who spent the most time in front of the television gained the most weight.

I'm sure you will not be surprised to learn that my "TV dinner" habit did nothing to alleviate my grief and sadness. The pain was all-consuming and I cried myself to sleep most nights. As bad as I felt, though, my unconscious eating made me feel even worse. I put on fifteen quick pounds. I began to notice how awful my stomach felt before bed. Mornings I would wake up feeling puffy all over. I didn't have control over many things at that point, but I finally realized that if I was to survive this ordeal I had to get a grip on the things I could control, and food was one of them.

I began following my own professional advice, which included planning my dinners during the day, when I felt less depressed. I would shop for dinner after eating a satisfying lunch. It is true what you've always heard: do not go to the grocery store when you're hungry, or you will be tempted to buy all the wrong foods. If possible, shop after you eat a satisfying meal.

Since most grocery stores offer a wide selection of choices, I eventually learned how to buy the proper amounts of healthy foods to create a fulfilling dinner for one. Fresh prepared foods from a salad bar or deli provided excellent solutions. If you live alone, lean deli meats, vegetable salads, hot soups, fresh-baked breads, and other ready-to-eat dishes offer simple, no-preparation answers for meals. While fried foods and heavy, sauce-laden specialties are often featured front and center in the deli case, be careful to splurge on them only occasionally.

Instead of watching television while eating dinner, I began listening to soothing music, which helped me consciously monitor my food quantities. Since the music calmed my nerves, it increased my appreciation of the various tastes that I had chosen earlier in the day.

Portions with Purpose

In Step One, I discussed the importance of nutritional balance and variety in meal choices. I also mentioned how the French love savoring every bite of food—but rarely gorge themselves. Portion size is really very important for achieving a healthier body, especially if you typically consume a steady stream of food unconsciously. Appropriate serving sizes can vary depending on your sex, age, size, level of activity, and other variables; however, to follow the Food Guide Pyramid, keep the following portion sizes in mind when preparing to eat.

Standard Serving Portions

Bread, cereal, rice, and pasta group (six to eleven servings a day)
One serving equals
One slice bread; one half roll or bagel; one 6" tortilla; one half-cup cooked rice, pasta, or oatmeal; one ounce cold cereal; one 4" pancake; two medium cookies

Vegetables group (three to five servings a day)
One serving equals
One half-cup chopped raw, non-leafy vegetables; one cup of leafy raw vegetables; one half-cup cooked veggies; one small baked potato; three-fourths cup vegetable juice

Fruit group (two to four servings a day)
One serving equals
One half-cup berries or chopped fruit; one medium apple, orange, or banana; three-fourths cup fruit juice; one-fourth cup dried fruit

Dairy group (two to three servings a day)
One serving equals
One cup milk or yogurt; one and one-half ounces cheese; two-thirds cup ice cream

Meat, poultry, fish, dry beans, eggs, and nuts group (two to three servings a day)
One serving equals
Two to three ounces cooked lean meat, poultry, fish, or sliced deli meat (which translates to one half hamburger patty, one half chicken breast, two slices deli meat); two to three ounces canned tuna or salmon (one half-cup); one half-cup cooked lentils, peas, or dry beans; one egg; two tablespoons peanut butter

Tips for Conscious, Healthy Eating Whether You Dine Alone or Not:

Whether you are divorced, widowed, a student, or simply choose to live alone, here are my suggestions for creating a healthier, more enjoyable meal experience. These same suggestions apply if you dine with others:

- Shop for dinner during the day when you have a full stomach.
- Buy delicious fresh-prepared foods so you don't have to cook for one (save fried or sauce-laden foods only for rare occasions).
- Plan dinner as if you are sharing the experience with someone else, i.e., set a place mat, napkin, and silverware, pour yourself a glass of wine and/or a glass of water, light a candle or place a flower in a bud vase on the table. I also like to say a silent prayer or affirmation before I begin eating.
- Place the appropriate serving sizes onto your plate before you sit down to dine. Don't set the entire container of pasta salad on the table, otherwise you'll be tempted to nibble on extra calories after your plate is empty.
- Direct your full attention to savoring your dinner; don't answer the phone or door during your meal.
- Soothing, enjoyable music is a wonderful dinner companion, but television, radio, newspapers, books, and other distractions are not.
- Try to eat dinner before 9 P.M., ensuring that this is the last food you consume for the night.
- Try to spend at least thirty minutes enjoying the meal (the longer, the better).
- After your meal is complete, don't simply rush out the door, on to your next activity. Give yourself a few minutes to enjoy the "glow" of a good meal by doing something fairly sedentary: reading, listening to music or radio, or yes, even watching television. (If there is a program being aired during your meal that you want to watch, tape it and watch it when you are finished eating.)

The following tips are specifically directed at super-moms who have a tendency to view meals as a small blip in the day between doctor appointments and basketball practice:

- Insist that the family gather for at least one meal a day, whether it's breakfast, dinner, or lunch. Studies have shown that successful, well-adjusted teenagers often eat at least one meal a day with the rest of the family.
- Emphasize variety, nutrition, and family preferences over what you're "supposed" to serve for a given meal. For example, who says sandwiches are only for lunch? Or eggs and pancakes are only for breakfast?
- Don't turn your dining table into a buffet table or a battlefield. Offer a healthy choice of foods and back off. What's the use of forcing your four-year-old to gag down broccoli if everyone's lost their appetite by the time the war is over?
- Enlist your family to help clear the table and wash the dishes, while you take a few minutes to let your meal settle.

There Are No Gold Medals for Speed Eating

The next time you're invited to a dinner party, take note of how quickly each guest finishes his or her meal. Invariably, there is the diner whose plate is already clean, just as someone across the table is beginning their entrée. Now note the eating demeanor of each of those guests. It's my experience that the more relaxed diner seems to take special pleasure in each morsel, setting down the fork between bites, sometimes engaging in light conversation, often making comments to the chef on each new taste and texture. Meanwhile, the speed demon often conveys an air of desperation, inhaling one mouthful after another, rarely joining discussions. You almost expect the beep of a stopwatch when he or she finally places the fork on the plate. Guess which style of eater is more often overweight?

I was first made aware of this phenomenon while eating with my oldest sister, Sudie. She is the quintessential poetic eater, grateful for every taste and sensation, always taking breaks between mouthfuls. I have never been able to eat as slowly as she does, yet I will always strive to meet her eating beat. Sudie's figure is a testament to her eating style. She has a body to die for, yet rarely exercises or turns down a taste that she desires. The fact is, she eats v-e-r-y slowly, recognizes when her stomach is satisfied, and stops when she's full. I have never known Sudie to overeat or be on a diet; she would never sacrifice the joy that eating brings her.

Another example is my friend Juana—one of the few people who can actually make eating a seductive experience. Why? Because she does it slowly and deliberately, exuding awareness and appreciation with each bite. Juana even moans like a happy pet when she eats certain foods, causing many a dinner companion to fall in love with her. She also has a stunning figure, and has never been on a diet in her life.

Eating slowly gives your body a very important opportunity: the opportunity to register and relay fullness to other critical organs—like the brain. When you're quickly stuffing yourself with food, your body's monitoring systems can't keep up. By the time the "full" message kicks in, you've already consumed another two pints of ice cream and half a bag of pretzels. But by taking more time as you eat, you give your body's natural regulator a chance to work. Gulping down food often means you're also gulping down air, which can lead to gas and indigestion. Eating slowly means you're chewing food better, and taxing your digestive system less. In addition, by consuming water during your meals (Step Two), your body will have a quicker understanding of the sensation of fullness. Try it—you'll be surprised how satisfied you feel, sooner, when you eat deliberately and slowly while drinking water in between conscious bites.

Sudie and Juana also taught me that being happy in your body has everything to do with how you eat, and why you eat. Those two women enjoy life. Similar to the European women I mentioned earlier, they eat for pleasurable nourishment, never missing an opportunity to enjoy great food. An essential element to living a healthy, balanced life is to be happy and to experience joy. When you eat with awareness, you increase your opportunity to savor not only food, but life.

How do you know if you're eating too fast? Do you put down your fork only after the meal is complete? Do you finish dinner in less than thirty minutes? Are you often gulping down meals between activities? Do you ever eat standing over the kitchen sink? I think you know what a "yes" answer to any of these questions means.

Say it again. "I will observe and decide what to eat, then enjoy my choices with awareness."

As you will see with my next story, eating with awareness will help you understand how to manage your weight problem. If eating isn't a joyous occasion, you have something in common with far more people than you realize. If you struggle to remember what you ate for dinner last night, you will appreciate knowing Anna.

Anna's Story

I first met Anna while I was lecturing at Canyon Ranch Health Spa. Although she arrived late to my lecture and sat in the back row, she stood out because of her attentiveness. After the lecture, she introduced herself, and we continued talking for the better part of an hour. One of the first things Anna shared was that she was fed up with trying to lose weight. She weighed more than she ever had, and was desperate for relief. Her eyes began to tear up when she spoke, saying that what she had heard of my talk made her feel like I could somehow help her. She wanted to know if we could schedule an appointment before the weekend ended. We met the following morning.

Anna is barely five feet tall and she admitted that her weight had surpassed the 150-pound mark. Her ideal weight, she said, was 110 pounds. As she talked about being 110 pounds, she referred to herself in the third person. She described a woman who was free, confident, and unencumbered. The 150-pound-plus woman sitting in front of me, however, spoke in the first person, giving vague excuses for her weight gain. While her words gave little indication as to what was going on inside of her, Anna's body language told me that she was a desperately unhappy woman. The only time she brightened was when she talked about her job, where it seemed she felt most comfortable and was very successful. However, she also expressed feelings of guilt about the amount of time she spent at her job, fearing she was not being a good mother to her three children.

While Anna was initially reluctant to share her inner emotions, a few pointed questions about food, exercise, and lifestyle brought tears and a river of pent-up pain and distress. The way the words came tumbling out made me suspect that her feelings had been buried a long time, and that unconscious eating was part of the problem. However, her willingness to open up showed me that Anna was ready to address these difficult issues.

Because she lived in Alabama, we agreed to weekly e-mail and phone sessions. Her first assignment was to send me a food journal of everything she ate for the next week.

When the e-mail arrived, and I read her entries, it didn't look as if she had eaten enough food to survive two days. I wondered how such a minimal number of calories had sustained her for an entire week.

When she called for her phone session, I asked if she had sent me her entire food journal for the week before. She responded that she had, yet she admitted having trouble at the end of the day remembering what she had eaten. I soon learned that meals were not happy times for Anna. She felt constantly rushed and harassed while trying to feed breakfast and dinner to herself, children, and husband. When I asked about lunch, she said she was usually too busy and instead munched on whatever food was available around the office. I asked what this included. Anna said, "I don't know . . . like chips or vending machine food, I guess. Maybe candy or nuts."

At the end of our phone conversation, I asked her to record her next week's entries immediately after eating them, so as not to forget what she had eaten. Anna was noticeably uncomfortable with this assignment, of which I made note.

The next week helped me understand more about how to help Anna. Her food journal was more complete, showing a scarcity of foods with protein, and an overabundance of carbohydrates and fat. I was proud of her for being honest.

During our phone session, she admitted that keeping a more accurate food journal had been quite an eye-opener. She noticed that she had eaten the same things most days. Writing it down also helped her recognize that most evenings included a late night snack while watching TV, hours after finishing a full dinner. Anna knew that snacking was not a good idea; however, she justified it by saying that it was her only quiet time away from the stresses in her life. She described it as her time to "veg out" with the nurturing relief of comfort food and mindless TV.

Late-night snacking is a common thread among overweight people, especially those who are unhappy. Anna admitted that she wasn't receiving meaningful companionship or support from her husband, Billy, and that she hadn't felt happy in the marriage for years. Ironically, Billy was a well-known chef; however, he rarely seemed interested in cooking for the family. Anna couldn't remember the last time she and Billy had enjoyed a quiet meal together. Food had become both Billy's and Anna's best friend, but one they shared separately. When your life becomes as unfulfilling as Anna's, food, no matter how unconsciously consumed, becomes a comfort. Unfortunately, while eating ultimately does nothing to fill your emotional voids, it will fill you with unnecessary calories and excess weight, adding to your despair.

I explained to Anna that she needed to make a conscious decision not to eat after 9 P.M., and to never eat while watching TV. I advised her to drink lots of water instead (Step Two). She agreed to try.

The next week, Anna was eager to tell me that she had not snacked after dinner, or while watching TV. But as a result of losing this crutch, she admitted feeling even more sadness than before. Instead of eating, she found herself crying most nights. I asked her what feelings came up when she cried. She blurted out, "I'm terrified that I don't love Billy anymore."

Her clarity was striking, but not unexpected. I suggested to Anna that perhaps her unconscious, late-night snacking had been blocking her true emotions and feelings. She started to cry, admitting that she had no idea what to do. First, I advised her to consult with a therapist to better understand how to proceed with her marriage. Second, I told her how essential it was to continue on her *Feel Good Naked* path, in order to learn that she had choices in her life that she could control.

Anna mentioned that the only thing she hated more than her body in clothes was the prospect of seeing her body out of clothes. She never looked at herself naked in the mirror, but she admitted to weighing herself every day, and shared that she had now passed the 155-pound mark. She could no longer fit into most of her clothes, and had been wearing the same three outfits—the only ones that fit—for the past year. She admitted staring longingly at her clothes that she wore when she was 110, 120, 130, and 140 pounds.

For the next week, in addition to keeping her food journal, I gave Anna several new assignments. They included to:

- Stop weighing herself. This is good advice for all women. Scales are the enemy of the *Feel Good Naked* lifestyle. They are all about absolute numbers that have little to do with how you look. Forget your scales. Throw them away. You can weigh-in annually at your doctor's office. The best gauge of how you look is how you feel naked.
- Give the clothes that she wore when she weighed 110 and 120 pounds to a charity.
- Stand in front of the mirror naked once a day.

- Record in her food journal the distinct flavors and textures of the foods she was eating. Could she detect certain spices or seasonings? Which were her favorites? Did she prefer crunchy foods or smooth, satiny textures? What foods complemented each other? We both knew this would help her pay closer attention to the food choices she was making.

I asked Anna if she could also find ten minutes each day for some kind of aerobic movement. She replied that she had absolutely no time for physical fitness, and that even if she had the desire to exercise, which she didn't, there was no room in her schedule for working out. I let the subject drop, knowing the impressive effort Anna was already putting into her program.

Over the next six months, several profound things happened to Anna. She began twice-a-week counseling and, among other insights, realized that her marriage was not salvageable. Billy, who had been suffering through his own mental anguish, agreed that the marriage was dead. They agreed to work diligently to share the responsibilities of raising their children.

Even though Anna's divorce was emotionally wrenching, she was experiencing a newfound energy and actually felt hopeful about getting through her trials and tribulations. She realized that the loneliness she had been living through in her dead marriage was much more painful than the reality of living without her husband.

She stopped weighing herself every day, and took immense pleasure in throwing away her scales. Anna gave her "skinny clothes" to charity, and expressed huge relief in not being reminded of her leaner days every time she looked in her closet.

She finally mustered the courage to look at herself naked in the mirror, and while there was some shock, Anna was also pleasantly surprised. As with most of us, her mind's image of her nude body was much worse than what the mirror revealed.

Anna realized that her careless, frenzied approach to meals, coupled with late-night snacking, had caused her to gain more than forty pounds. Had she not discovered Step Five, she might have easily packed on another hundred pounds. Step Five taught Anna how to eat consciously, not allowing food to mask her emotions. Instead, she gained comfort in adopting a diet of honesty, choice, and awareness.

As Anna gained control over her life, she was able to deal with her dietary imbalances (Step One). As well, she eventually allowed me to help her develop a new approach to time management, freeing up regular time for movement and exercise (Step Four). Anna also discovered the importance of "personal time" in her life (Step Eight). She learned to honor this time and plan for it as she would any fun outing, instead of collapsing in front of the television and spending her time in "default" mode. Finally, Anna realized it was time to give her children the attention she had been giving her job. She cut back her work schedule to three days a week, and committed to leaving her office promptly at 5 P.M., no matter what her work load.

Fast-forward two years. Here's an update on Anna.

Her current weight is 128 pounds, which she has maintained for several months. She only allows herself to be weighed during her annual visit to her gynecologist. She looks at herself naked with complete comfort, preferring morning time on an empty stomach. This ritual has become her new set of scales. She also monitors her weight by the fit of her clothes. Both of these methods give Anna a feeling of control, yet neither create anxiety or stress. Anna and her ex-husband have found amicable footing on which to share custody and responsibility for raising their children. She reports a gratifying feeling of fulfillment being more involved in her children's lives. For the past six months, Anna has been dating a man she met at work. They enjoy dining out and trying new restaurants together. In order to not regain her lost weight, she has successfully utilized my *Feel Good Naked* restaurant survival tips. These tips include:

- Never arrive at a restaurant famished. If you are really hungry, eat a light snack before you go out to eat (a small container of nonfat yogurt or a banana usually abates my hunger).
- If bread is brought to your table first, ask that it not be served until the meals are presented.
- If you eat and enjoy meat, try to order entrées that are grilled, broiled, roasted, or braised with herbs and seasonings—which don't add fat or calories—instead of meats that are fried or cooked in rich sauces.
- If it's not listed on the menu, ask when ordering how each dish is prepared. Avoid dishes that include extra butter or cream sauces. Don't be afraid to ask for a substitution of steamed vegetables for a high-calorie side dish. Save the french fries for special occasions.
- When ordering salad, ask for the dressing to be very light (this is better than applying it yourself since your portion is probably heavier than a light sprinkling from the kitchen).
- If there are "light meals" available, take advantage of this option. Eat only a standard portion amount of each food on your plate, asking for the remainder to be boxed to take home. Another way to limit portion size is to order from the appetizer menu, although this can result in a meal of limited variety.
- Eat slowly. Put your fork down on the plate after each bite.
- Drink lots of water.
- If you enjoy alcohol with your meal, try to stick to wine. A typical five-ounce glass of dry wine has 100 calories. A twelve-ounce wine cooler, however, has 180 calories, and a twelve-ounce mug of beer has 150 calories. Mixed drinks, especially those with soft drink mixers, can contain 300 calories or more. Cordials or liqueurs contain 160 calories for every one and one-half ounces.
- Enjoy dessert, but ask yourself if you really need the whipped cream or other additional toppings. Sorbet is a wonderful dessert choice, or share dessert with your dinner companion(s).
- Enjoy yourself and don't be shy about asking for alterations to menu listings. Remember, you are paying for your meal.

Anna now makes a concerted effort to eat three balanced, conscious meals each day. She doesn't dawdle at breakfast, she does sit down to eat with her children. She packs a hearty lunch at home, and brings it with her to work. Anna also enjoys a healthy afternoon mini-meal, which keeps her from speed snacking when she gets home from work. At dinner, she eats particularly slowly and deliberately, knowing that this will be her last food intake for the day.

Anna continues to keep a daily food journal. This ritual keeps her honest. She also uses her journal for venting emotions. If Anna feels sad, mad, lonely, neglected, or frustrated, she acknowledges and faces her emotions, instead of running to food as a cover-up. And, on those rare occasions when she decides to indulge in something decadent, she decides what her choices will be, sets them out, and indulges with awareness (Step One). When her treat is finished, she stops.

Anna tells me that the main difference in her life since incorporating my ten-step program has been spending time with herself consciously, in order to understand her strengths and weaknesses, her emotions, and what she needs to be happy. She has dared to know herself, which has taught her how to eat with awareness and not use food as an emotional crutch.

Summary:

Step Five is devoted to helping you become aware and purposeful in your eating habits, giving your full attention to this joyful ritual, instead of letting it become a mindless gesture. For Anna, this awareness started when she began keeping a food journal, recording her entries as soon as she ate them.

Without food to fill the emotional void in Anna's life, she was able to confront her long-suppressed feelings—feelings that were preventing her from moving forward and finding happiness in her life. She learned that confronting these feelings and taking action was less painful than the unhappiness of avoiding them. Once she was no longer using food to mask her emotions, she was able to embrace and appreciate eating as a celebration of nourishment.

Anna was obsessed with weighing herself each day, which caused her moods to fluctuate depending on whether or not the number went up or down. She learned that a better measure of her general health and well-being was how she looked in the mirror naked. She only weighs herself once a year at the doctor's office. Throwing away her scales and giving her too-small clothes to charity was satisfying and liberating.

Anna also understands the importance of carving out personal time for herself, in order to listen to what's going on in her head and heart. She realizes the power of the mind-body connection and that she can't cheat one without having an impact on the other.

To enjoy the full benefits of Step Five, start keeping a food journal of everything you consume. This will give you an honest account of your daily consumption. When you eat, don't allow distractions such as TV or newspapers. Instead, eat mindfully, involving all of your senses. Don't eat to avoid difficult feelings. If you're sad, cry. If you're angry, get mad. Then move on to finding solutions that will ease your pain.

As you become aware of the food you're eating, be mindful of the portions you consume—make sure they're within the guidelines of "standard" servings which have been outlined in the Food Guide Pyramid. Allow enough time to eat so your meals can be unhurried and leisurely, and slow down your eating pace so your body can tell when it's full.

Eating with awareness is the best way to avoid overeating. Whether eating with family or friends, or enjoying a quiet meal alone, remember that moderation is balance, and balance promotes joy. Learn and repeat the phrase "I will observe and decide what to eat, then enjoy my choices with awareness."

STEP **6**

PICK AN IDOL AND LET THAT PERSON MOTIVATE YOU.

Follow Your Heart's Desire

We all need inspiration in our lives. Music, religion, pictures, poetry, people—whatever our muses, they fuel our progress and keep us going when life conspires against us.

Whenever I begin working with new clients, I ask them to complete a short background profile that includes the questions:

- Whose physical appearance would you like to have, and why?
- Whom do you admire, and why?
- What are your dreams and aspirations?

Ask yourself these three questions and then write down your answers.

Imitation Is the Most Sincere Form of Flattery

In many ways, the first question is the most important. Wait a minute, you may be thinking, why promote lusting after a "look" or a body you were never meant to have? Isn't that the type of unrealistic thinking we're trying to avoid with the *Feel Good Naked* lifestyle?

Yes . . . and no. Being completely honest and writing down your own personal "gold standard" in terms of appearances can reveal some interesting things. For example, I can't tell you how many large-boned women long for a petite frame. Or how many small women wish they looked like "Xena, Warrior Princess." The truth is, you can wish for a vastly different body type until the cows come home—but it's not going to happen. By admitting your desire, however, you can begin to see the physical impossibility of it—and start bringing your goals for your body more in line with what is possible.

That's where hope gets kindled. Okay, so you'll never have the body of Cindy Crawford. But what about that teacher at your son's school—the one who's short like you, but always seems to look about five inches taller than she really is? The one with the hip haircut and quick smile? Now there's someone you wouldn't mind looking more like. And the good news is, you can.

Of course, that's not to say that famous bodies can't motivate you. When I think about Linda Hamilton's arms in *Terminator 2*, I exercise my arms more effectively. When I think about Madonna's concentrated dance movements, I dance better. When I think about Demi Moore's body in *Indecent Proposal*, I run farther. When I envision Oprah Winfrey's before and after photographs, I realize I am not too tired to work out after all.

The important thing is to find a look you can aspire to that won't set you up for failure. Embrace a vision of what you'd like to become, remembering that it can be anyone from anywhere. Attach a picture of your physical role model to your refrigerator or bathroom mirror. Allow her image to inspire you. Change the picture occasionally so that when you feel down, your idol's image can help refresh your motivation. Creating the visual fantasy, then envisioning yourself as the fantasy, is half the work of making it come true. Visualization is a key tool to feeling good naked.

My inspirational pictures include:

Madonna. For sheer over-the-top, no-holds-barred energy and body savvy no one can touch Madonna. She has provided me with two decades of creative energy and inspiration. For all the superfluous hoopla that swirls around her, Madonna's body is a testament to the power of her focus and determination. Like her or not, she constantly reminds us that believing in ourselves can take us anywhere. I can tell you confidently that Madonna feels good naked and revels in it.

Oprah Winfrey. Oprah's very public struggle with her body issues are an inspiration to me. Despite her high-profile celebrity, she's never been afraid to reveal her personal fears and challenges—helping millions of women who share her battles. Oprah's triumphs and even her setbacks motivate and help me to dig deeper for inner strength. She is an icon, a pioneer, and a woman who reminds me time and time again to never allow others to diminish my power.

Use Inspiring Stories, People, and Virtues to Propel Your Power

The second and third questions are less about appearance and more about character and achievement. All three questions are designed to guide you toward a more confident, motivated, and inspired you, while creating harmony between your body, mind, and spirit.

Among the qualities that I value and admire in people are honesty, determination, strength, integrity, and vibrancy. When I recognize these standards in others, it motivates me to work on the same characteristics in myself. In turn, when I'm feeling good about who I am as a person, I'm more encouraged to have my outside look as good as I feel inside.

Striving for excellence while reaching to become the best people we can be is intoxicating, magical stuff. It spills into every aspect of our lives, and feeds our morality on every level.

Those whom I admire include:

Lance Armstrong. I'm wildly inspired by stories and people like Lance Armstrong, who overcame a dire cancer prognosis to win cycling's premier event, the Tour de France. Lance's remarkable comeback from testicular cancer is a constant reminder that our minds are as powerful as our bodies. I am moved by his physical accomplishments. He helps diminish my fear of illness and physical setbacks. I am motivated by his intensity and his ability to overcome the unimaginable.

My two sisters. Throughout my life, Sudie and Chris have taught me the true meaning of friendship, love, honest communication, and courage. My sisters are the coolest women I will ever know. My mother and father gave me the greatest gift by making me a member of their tribe.

My husband. Roger is one of the few people I know who is brave enough to live a gutsy, honest life. He lives close to his soul, guiding his life with authenticity. He has inspired me creatively, by his own impressive career choices to be a photographer and a film director. In addition, I have never known a more attentive, gifted parent.

My dreams and aspirations are:

Mentally: To expand my brain, always questioning and challenging my limits. To continue sharing lessons and discoveries that I believe can help others. To write for the rest of my days.

Physically: To be more balanced each decade of my life, remaining active everyday. To choreograph a live *Feel Good Naked* dance revue that would appear off-Broadway in New York City. To practice yoga regularly, and to celebrate my ninetieth birthday doing a sensuous tango.

Soulfully: To direct my days with clear intentions and authenticity. To forget fear. To help others. To continue to mother my stepsons from the deepest source of instinct that I know.

Who do you admire? Why? What are your dreams and aspirations? Write these things down, take them seriously, and hold them constantly in front of you. They are not out of reach, as long as they're not out of your mind's eye.

I Wish I May, I Wish I Might

After my parents' divorce, I visited my father at his apartment whenever possible. Unlike in today's culture of divorce, where schedules are organized between two households in advance, overnights with my father were infrequent and spontaneous. I would have preferred to spend more time with him; however, because he lived a footloose bachelor's life, my mother rarely brought me to his house for sleepovers. When I did spend the night, he took me everywhere with him, including the French Quarter of New Orleans. I lived for these adventures and the way they made me feel—so grown-up and worldly. I remember thinking how weird it was to feel as wise as I did at the age of twelve. I wanted more life experiences than those made available by my mother. My dad seemed to understand this, going out of his way to honor my maturity, encouraging my individuality. Times shared with him taught me much about my personal power, my unique beauty, and my dreams.

One of my dad's favorite places was the Louis XIV Hotel. We would go there to hear the Johnny Bachman Trio perform. It was thrilling to be there and I felt electrified inside while listening to their chic renditions of Stevie Wonder, Carly Simon, or Louis Armstrong. I could feel the deep rhythms throughout my entire body. I fantasized about being on stage with Johnny and the band.

As I became a regular with my father, Johnny Bachman took a shining to me, as did other members of the audience. These men and women always seemed genuinely excited to see me. Instead of addressing me as a little girl, they would ask me adult questions, including me in their conversations, eager to know my opinions. In the notorious words of Sally Field, they liked me. They really, really liked me. It was one of the first times I felt socially respected and secure. I felt like I could do anything in their presence and still be accepted.

During one of Johnny's breaks, while he was conversing with Dad and me at our table, I confided in Johnny that my secret ambition was to sing with him. He asked me what song I would want to sing. I thought for a moment and came up with my favorite hit of the moment, "You Are the Sunshine of My Life." In the middle of the next set, much to my astonishment, Johnny's band broke into "You Are the Sunshine of My Life," and he invited me onstage to accompany him. What an unforgettable moment. Decades later, it is still fresh in my memory and remains a life-changing event. There I was, living my dream. After the song, the audience went wild. Johnny looked at me with a huge grin and asked, "So, Laure, what'll it be next?" I replied, "Let's do 'Hello Dolly.'" And away we went. I felt like the happiest person in the world, convinced that my life's calling was to stand up in front of people and perform.

What stands out in my mind today are the positive messages these men and women contributed to my then fragile self-image. Dad, Johnny, and the audience members all inspired me that night to follow my dreams and do what made me happy, however audacious. To never give in to the notion of what *should* make me happy. They taught me that if you can see and believe in your dreams, they can come true. You just need to go out and get them. Feeling safe enough to stand in front of a group and express myself prompted my choices later in life to guide and lead others. Each of us has a personal path. We just need to continue to believe in it, as our path unfolds before our eyes.

From Cher to Jane Fonda

During my adolescent years, with the memory of my brief but successful singing debut still fresh in my mind, I lived for the "Sonny and Cher" show. I would squeeze turtlenecks over my head backward to imitate Cher's luxurious long locks, while singing her songs with a hairbrush microphone. For the most part, those years were troubled, emotional, confused times as I battled my weight and struggled to overcome the break-up of our family. But when Cher and I got together—everything else melted away. Having her as an idol got me through countless rough times.

In my twenties, when I first saw Madonna's "Lucky Star" video, I remember being stunned by her physical power. She awakened me, because I could imagine myself doing what she was doing. I could move as well as she could, and I certainly had the nerve to perform. Since I already had my New York exercise studio, I was given the daily opportunity to live out these fantasies. To this day, I believe that one of the reasons I was a successful fitness instructor was because I would fantasize while teaching that I was in a Madonna video, and that my students were my back-up dancers. I believe this excitement was transferred to everyone in the room, creating a potent, energy-packed atmosphere.

When Madonna showed up at my studio for class I nearly fainted. Watching her do my moves was another life-changing moment. I still remember the way she funneled all of her focus and energy into each move. It was inspiring and made me work even harder.

During this same time, Jane Fonda's exercise videos were becoming very popular. I followed Fonda's videos, influenced by her enthusiasm and energy. As I studied her delivery on camera, I imagined myself in her shoes. The kernel of a dream was born.

Mary Tyler Moore as Mentor

Legendary actress Mary Tyler Moore began taking my exercise classes in 1985. When she first began attending my classes, I was struck by her posture, her sleek, defined muscles, and intense focus. Mary projects a startling combination of refinement and strength; whenever she was in class, everyone else worked harder. You simply cannot be in her presence without noticing her physical radiance.

Her ability to inspirit others had such a powerful effect on me that in 1993, I approached her about doing a series of exercise videos with me. To my excitement, she agreed, and I had the opportunity to spend a summer working daily with Mary, training her like an Olympic athlete. She, in turn, taught me about her own personal journey to a healthy relationship with her body.

There were many lessons that Mary's friendship taught me. First, I was introduced to a new level of self-discipline and strength. I thought I was self-motivated, but after spending time with one of America's most-loved celebrities, I discovered a new, enhanced version of self-propelled energy. As a young ballerina, Mary had developed the power and freedom of body awareness and the discipline of focus; these gifts had stayed with her throughout her life.

Second, she taught me how to physically and mentally embrace the stages of our body's aging process. Mary understands that she will never again have the body of a twenty-year-old. But she is always ready to challenge her body with something new. She is able to keep the dancer/athlete alive and stimulated within herself, which translates into amazing charisma and vivacity. For these reasons, she became one of my greatest inspirations and mentors.

Our video series was a success, but I gained so much more from the process than just a feather in my cap. I was able to combine a dream (of hosting an exercise video) with a role model (Mary Tyler Moore) to visualize a goal, fuel my motivation, and make it happen.

Joyce's Story

I met Joyce soon after I completed my video series with Mary. She approached me in the ladies' room at a restaurant where we were both dining.

Joyce said she had been watching me eat at the table next to hers, and when I got up to go to the restroom, she was impressed with my athletic body. She wanted to know if I was a professional dancer. She wanted to know how long I worked out every day, and if someone heavyset like her could be fit.

I told her I was a fitness therapist. She wanted to know what that meant. I explained that I worked with women on their body issues, guiding them toward healthier habits, while helping them find happiness through the integration of their body, mind, and spirit. Her reply was, "Sign me up." I hoped I could help her feel as much excitement about herself as she felt for me, a total stranger.

Our first meeting was at her home, which was a wonderful environment filled with bright artifacts from around the world. Joyce was single when we met, working brutal hours for a top Wall Street investment house. What immediately struck me about her personal surroundings were the colorful objects that seemed to define her passions for life. By the look and feel of her home, I would have guessed Joyce to be an artist or performer. Her space was pure creativity.

When she mentioned that she worked on Wall Street, I thought she was pulling my leg. I had known many number-crunchers, but none of whom had seemed as creative as Joyce.

When we got to the question about her dreams and aspirations, Joyce surprisingly steered the conversation to her acting stints in college, not her current life choices. She explained that her love of acting was what had motivated her to relocate from New Jersey to New York City. Yet, once living in the city, she was discouraged by the economic prospects of trying to make it as an actress. Disheartened, Joyce began interviewing for other jobs, and was offered a high-paying position in international finance. She decided to "grow up" and take a "real" job, abandoning her love of acting.

I learned that Wall Street had provided Joyce with more than money—along the way, she had gained so much weight that she now topped 200 pounds. Long work hours, frequent travel, and a love of rich foods had caused the scales to tip against Joyce—literally.

Her road to riches began and ended at a computer monitor, where she sat from early morning until late at night—often munching mindlessly—while watching the financial markets. Her exercise included raising her arm to hail taxis to and from work, and walking from her desk to the elevator. Besides fancy late-night dinners, Joyce's other meal choices usually included a high-fat muffin or bagel with cream cheese for breakfast, and maybe a piece of pizza or a tuna melt with fries for lunch. Except for dinner, most meals were eaten at her desk. Joyce never took breaks during her day, not even to walk outside for five minutes.

Despite her situation, though, Joyce was a delightfully upbeat person. She seemed genuinely accepting of the fact that she would never be skinny. However, she expressed real concern at having passed the 200-pound mark, and wanted to be at least healthy, if not thin.

Like most people, Joyce suffered from a lack of free time. She told me she couldn't spare more than two hours a week for my program. She refused to consider changing her eating habits, especially the dinners, which were often expense-account extravaganzas in the best restaurants of New York. She did agree to throw away her bathroom scale and to fill out my questionnaire. I went over the ten steps with her, left a background profile for Joyce to complete, and we agreed to meet the following week.

During our next meeting, we reviewed her answers to my questions. In addition to learning about Joyce's history, I also learned that . . .

She would like to look like: Liza Minelli.
She admired: her cousin Gabriella.
Her dreams and aspirations included the desire for:
• more time
• less stress
• less hierarchy
• less travel
• more theater, creativity, and passion

It became clear by our fourth meeting that as good as she was in finance, Joyce's professional life did little to satisfy her soul. In order for her to realize her true aspirations, she would need to honor her artistic desires in a more meaningful way. Joyce began to again consider the idea of finding work in the world of entertainment. Since her cousin Gabriella was a cabaret performer, Joyce agreed to meet with her to better understand the politics of New York's acting industry.

After meeting with Gabriella, and assessing the rewards of her Wall Street years, Joyce came to a remarkable realization: she could afford to maintain her current lifestyle for a full year without employment. The realization of this luxury fueled her courage, and she soon resigned from her finance job, while at the same time signing up for acting classes.

Within the first month of Joyce's new life, she had lost ten pounds. I attributed this loss to taking a walk three times a week in Central Park, and not eating junk food at her desk. Joyce attributed her weight loss to her newfound energy and optimism, and the remarkable reduction in her stress levels since leaving the world of business. She also believed her body was benefiting by not traveling. Joyce's Wall Street job required her to go overseas every third week of the month, and she firmly believed that airplane and hotel food had been a major culprit in her weight gain. Whatever the reasons, Joyce was already moving toward her dreams.

The next step of our weekly work together was to prepare Joyce for the difficult task of pursuing her goal of becoming an actress. Although she was thrilled to be venturing into this new career, she was petrified to imagine auditioning in her large body. She feared she would be rejected because of her size twenty-four physique.

My advice to Joyce revolved around building self-esteem. In order to do that, we compiled a list of larger women who are successful entertainers. The list included gifted performers such as Camryn Manheim, Aretha Franklin, and Kathy Bates. As we gathered the names, we realized how attractive big can be. Despite the fact that the media constantly projects thin as beautiful, it became apparent to Joyce that healthy self-confidence can define beautiful in today's world. Her goal was to continue to get healthier, while allowing the images of these Hollywood women to fuel her motivation. She taped pictures of them up in strategic places in her apartment.

Joyce began walking for a full hour four times each week. As she took each strong, purposeful stride, she would visualize herself walking with confidence and determination into her auditions—the same characteristics she imagined her Hollywood role models exhibited whenever they auditioned.

She also agreed to re-examine her eating habits. Since she no longer ate take-out breakfasts, lunches, or expense-account dinners, she decided to give Step One a try. Since Joyce had never had time or interest in dieting, she was happy to hear I didn't expect her to adhere to one now. But in the spirit of becoming healthier, she was open to making the effort to eat three balanced, nutritious meals a day. And she loved the fact that she could treat herself once a week.

To help Joyce embrace her acting ambition, I made a very unorthodox suggestion. I asked her to think about practicing for auditions naked. (Mind you, I didn't say to show up for auditions naked—to try practicing her lines at home in the nude.) I felt this would help reinforce the idea of projecting her whole glorious self into the roles she hoped to win. She was somewhat hesitant at first, but later confided to me that after the fear and anxiety she felt undressing to practice her lines, reading in front of casting directors seemed like a piece of cake. "If I can read the lines to myself naked, I can read them anywhere—to anyone," she concluded.

It worked. After three months, Joyce had lost thirty pounds, and scored her first acting job off-Broadway. Finally, she was being paid to do what she loved. As a result of her theatrical accomplishment, Joyce's self-confidence grew.

This was her lifetime dream, and she was living it. Achieving this goal propelled Joyce into auditioning for other roles, and within six months, she had found a reputable talent agent. The agent reassured Joyce to be who she was, not who she thought society expected her to be, and assured her that there was plenty of room in the acting world for true talent—regardless of physical size or appearance. She was right.

As Joyce continued to live a healthy life, attend acting classes, and show up for auditions, consistent acting work began rolling in the door. Her first television job came almost one year to the day after leaving her unsatisfying Wall Street job. Joyce was hired on a popular soap opera to play the part of a nurse who falls in love with a younger doctor. Ironically, the doctor winds up leaving an unfulfilling relationship to pursue his true love: Joyce's character. Joyce's soap opera job lasted a full year. When it ended, she was inundated with other wonderful television opportunities.

Two years later, Joyce relocated to Los Angeles, where her agent believed her television recognition would grow. Again, the agent's hunch was accurate.

Today, ten years later, Joyce still lives in Los Angeles. She is married to a theater director, and I see her regularly on television. She is a happy size fourteen and cannot imagine a day without a long walk. Joyce calls herself a big, beautiful woman. On those days when she feels down and out, she watches Oprah on television for inspiration and motivation. Joyce continues to realize the power of mentors and how they can inspire her to follow her dreams and achieve her goals. She also never forgets how dead her life felt fifty pounds ago. Although she feels like her Wall Street days were another lifetime ago, she also talks about the importance of remembering that time. Joyce knows that without that experience, she never would have been able to find the *Feel Good Naked* lifestyle—or the courage to follow her heart's desire.

Summary:

Rather than listening to her heart and the dreams she harbored to be an actress, Joyce submitted to pursuing the conventional career she thought she *should* have. While it was not a "wrong" decision—it eventually provided her with the economic freedom to pursue her dreams—Joyce's body and health paid a price. Discovering role models for her unconventional aspirations helped her find her way back to a creative career, giving her the courage to pursue and achieve her goals.

Whether it is your sister, neighbor, Mary Tyler Moore, or Madonna, pick a physical role model and allow that person to motivate you to live a healthier life. Choose someone whose body type is not impossibly different from yours—remember, you can't change genetics. Once you have a role model, start visualizing yourself with some of their physical attributes—a straighter posture, slimmer thighs, a ready smile, self-confidence.

Also focus on the non-physical qualities you admire in others and would like to enhance in yourself. The better you feel about who you are as a person, the easier it will be to motivate a physical transformation. For Joyce, it was about choosing successful, larger-sized actresses whom she could mentally aspire to emulate.

Believe in your dreams. Spend more time looking forward, not back. Don't let fear paralyze you—if you can dream it, it can happen. But you must have the courage of your convictions and the willingness to take action, even risks. That's how your idol did it. Now it's your turn.

STEP 7

BREATHE CONSCIOUSLY FOR FIVE MINUTES EVERY DAY.

I Am Barely Breathing

In the feature film, *Ever After*, Drew Barrymore's character freezes at a crucial life-changing moment, anticipating what's about to happen. She is paralyzed with fear and is reduced to her most basic instincts. She closes her eyes, and softly whispers to herself, "Just breathe."

It's worth noting: when our mental and reasoning capabilities fail, we find ourselves at the mercy of our bodies' most elemental functions. Of those functions, none is more essential than breathing. You could say that breathing is life.

Unfortunately, breath awareness seems most prevalent in moments of fear or panic. It is not until our hearts pound and our lungs jump that we notice our shortened inhale, followed by our hollow exhale.

Fortunately, the importance of breathing is gaining recognition, with the increased popularity of mind-body exercises such as yoga, Pilates, and stretching. All of these practices focus on the fundamentals of breathing. People who regularly run, bike, or swim are also aware of the necessity of conscious breathing. But whether you are active or inactive, you can benefit from the transforming experience of putting your lungs to work.

What exactly is conscious breathing? It's really just another term for deep breathing. Breathing deeply and slowly for five minutes each day is one of the most effective ways to receive the full benefits of our amazing respiratory system, while minimizing stress. It is at the heart of relaxation, offering a surprisingly simple option for physical and psychological self-healing. Breathing in, we flood our bodies with the vital oxygen our red blood cells need to function optimally. Breathing out, we rid ourselves of carbon dioxide waste. I once heard breathing referred to as the preventive medicine of the twenty-first century.

On pages 104–105 in *The Spirited Walker*, author Carolyn Kortge explains that "conscious breathing energizes the body, calms the emotions, and sharpens the mind, providing our bodies with a natural source of alertness, vitality, and health. Researchers say it also slows the loss of vital lung capacity that often accompanies aging. As you breathe in fresh oxygen, you bring vital resources to the cells of the body and preserve the elasticity of lung tissue. You protect your capacity to live life fully. At the same time, production of carbon dioxide mounts as cells flush out waste products. Full exhalation releases spent resources that linger in the base of the lungs. When you breathe with awareness, each breath unites you with the power of life that surrounds and sustains you."

Each of us breathes somewhere in the vicinity of seventeen-thousand times every day, but very few of those breaths are deep, slow, effective breaths that can improve the function of our lungs, organs, and circulatory system, all the way down to the cellular level.

What's more, not only is effective deep breathing advantageous, but too-shallow breathing (the way most of us breathe, most of the time) has been linked to physical ills such as headaches and high blood pressure. Researchers have also found that shallow, rapid breathing can trigger our nervous system's fight-or-flight response, which can make us feel anxious and exhausted.

Besides enhancing our day-to-day health, conscious deep breathing can help us tap into what's going on inside of us—wants, needs, the small but wise voice that is often drowned out in the noise of everyday life. I wish I had known this simple truth before entering my first marriage.

True Confessions of an Unconscious Breather

My first husband and I were together for a total of five years, two of them married. I think he would agree it was ultimately a disaster, although of course neither of us went into it thinking it would turn out that way. During the time we were together, I rarely practiced a regular conscious breathing ritual, although I preached its benefits to my clients. It was great—for others. Personally, I had neither the time nor need for it. Wrong.

Michael and I first started bumping into each other around the neighborhood on New York's Upper West Side. Before we officially met, we had noticed each other in various locations, but had never spoken. I first noticed his good looks at a favorite sauna. I would go there twice a month to sit in my bathing suit in this big room with twenty others, absorbing temperatures that exceeded 200 degrees. When you felt light-headed from the high temperatures, you would pour buckets of freezing cold water over your head, causing one of the most extraordinary physical and mental sensations. I always noticed Michael doing yoga in these hot temperatures. His gaze captured mine and I wondered who he was.

Over the next three years, I would see him: at a bar in Soho, hailing a taxi-cab on the Upper East Side, in a restaurant in Tribeca, and countless times at the sauna. Finally one fateful night, there we were, yet again, walking toward each other on Columbus Avenue. We both stopped, while laughing, asking, "Who are you?" He asked me to join him for sushi, which I did, and from that moment on, I knew we would affect each other's lives.

Michael was an investment banker who would rather have chosen a job in the arts. I have never known a man with better taste. Over the next two years, he introduced me to incredible New York restaurants, Bergdorf Goodman's department store, champagne and caviar, Chilean poet Pablo Neruda, unbelievable lingerie, astounding jewelry, beautiful clothes, Paris, and Santa Fe. He constantly wined and dined me, giving me gifts with soul-baring notes that included romantic quotes from fine writers. I was quickly hooked, lost in the rhythm of our romance. At this point in my life, I had never had a man want to please me so much. Life became a fun, magical whirlwind that felt great.

Michael proposed in Provence, France, after showing me Paris. Then he swept me away to the beaches of the Mediterranean. Three weeks later, we returned to Manhattan engaged and ready to live together. Although I agreed to cohabitation, I wanted to wait a year to be married. It was a wild year; my television career began to take off, and my concerns about Michael began to grow. There were problematic signs around the issues of money and loyalty; bills were never paid on time and he always checked out other women while dining with me. Nevertheless, I tuned out that voice of reason.

Eventually, without the rose-colored excitement of courtship, more differences in our values and opinions emerged. I sensed our connection was dwindling, but ignored my doubts. I convinced myself that since we enjoyed working out together, eating together, going to the theater and traveling, we should move ahead with our plans to marry.

Once married, Michael's attentiveness waned even more. Within the first few months, differing opinions were impossible to ignore, and our communication became angry and destructive. Because each of us felt attacked, we fell into defensive postures that compounded with each passing day. As our conflicts mounted, I also began to suspect that Michael might be living a private life. His whereabouts became sketchier and sketchier.

We saw a marriage counselor; however, no therapist could have pulled us out of our embarrassing power struggle. Our marriage had become like a horrible episode of "People's Court." I no longer felt safe in his presence; instead, I was overwhelmed with feelings of disrespect and distrust. I had grown intolerant of the way he drove, spoke to waiters and waitresses, lost his temper, didn't pay bills, spoke to his mother, spoke to me, looked away when I spoke, didn't ask me any questions, didn't listen, didn't care.

When in Doubt, Breathe

Despite our massive problems, I kept telling myself this was the "or worse" of "for better or worse." I believed we would somehow snap out of our hard times. I wanted desperately to recapture the fairy-tale romance of our initial courtship, yet was constantly being confronted with evidence that the fairy tale had turned into a nightmare. I began to find receipts from places I had never heard of or been to. When I was working out of town, Michael would never be home for our scheduled phone calls. And toward the end of our relationship, he would tell me he was going to a meeting in one location, yet when I called, nobody knew who I was talking about. When I confronted him, he told me I was paranoid and crazy and needed more counseling.

The night I unexpectedly walked in on him in bed with another woman was certainly the most shocking moment of my life. In many respects, it was a great relief—I was not crazy or paranoid after all. Once again, I learned the invaluable lesson of trusting the small voice inside.

This incident, perhaps the most devastating of all human experiences, was one that I never would have imagined I could survive. But I did. In that moment of abject horror, I was reduced to basic body functions. As my ability to think clearly slipped away, my body fell into a "default state," reverting to the calming, meditative breathing I had promoted to others for so many years. It was a lifeline I will always be thankful for.

It suddenly became clear that I had been clinging ridiculously to an image of Michael that had nothing to do with who Michael really was. In fact, I knew very little about the man I was married to. I did know that he was a liar. And I immediately knew I wanted a divorce. Oddly, Michael didn't. He ignored my lawyer's calls, and refused to vacate our shared living space. I moved in with a friend and eventually got my divorce. Our "People's Court" had finally ended. My healing had just begun.

To be strong enough to walk out of an unbearable marriage had everything to do with my self-love. While I was by no means impervious to the heartache and emotional devastation such trauma brings, the groundwork I had laid in my previous work to strengthen and balance my body—and my life—was invaluable in realizing that I deserved better than such abusive treatment.

Over the next few weeks, I relied on conscious breathing many times as I fought through constant numbness and terror. I developed a mantra that seemed to help: "When in doubt, breathe." I repeated this any time I felt incapable of moving forward. It always brought about a subtle change, first in my physical state, eventually in my mental perspective, allowing me to take another step ahead. I wished that I had begun practicing this simple ritual before an emotional trauma made it necessary. I'm certain the insight it brings could have helped avert disaster much sooner.

Nothing can amply prepare us for death, divorce, adultery, deceit, abuse, or deep heartache. However, if you have worked to achieve balance and acceptance in your body, mind, and spirit, you will never have to question your self-worth in these desperate life moments. And if you have given your body a mechanism for dealing with difficult times—like the gift of conscious breathing—you will be forever grateful when those tough times arise.

Practice Conscious Breathing for Five Minutes. Enjoy the Benefits for Twenty-four Hours.

Three months after the Bedroom Incident, the immediate terror and trauma of the moment had begun to fade. I moved into my own apartment, and felt comforted by the serenity of a new home. Yet I still felt constantly nervous and out of sorts. I feared that I would never enjoy life, or laughter, again. Many mornings I awoke with a pounding heartbeat, gripped by anxiety and fear.

Since breathing had been such an important part of my initial coping stage, I decided to do even more breathing to see if it could help my anxiety. I made daily five-minute breathing meditations a priority, sometimes engaging in these five-minute sessions three or four times a day. Even with my background in meditation, I had never felt such dramatic results. As soon as I started, I could feel the stress melt away. I knew that relaxation reduces blood pressure levels, and during this stressful time, mine was definitely high.

Slowly but surely, this simple five-minute breathing ritual helped me live courageously again. As well, it reminded me:

- how to take action in the presence of fear
- how to renew my daily focus
- how to balance and trust my instincts and choices
- how to manage doubt and insecurity

Here is the routine I continue to use in my five-minute conscious-breathing ritual:

1) I sit up in my bed, with my back against the wall for spinal awareness and support, legs comfortably crossed, eyes closed, hands resting comfortably on my knees, palms turned upward. You may be more comfortable sitting in a chair with your feet on the floor or lying on your back; adapt your position to what works best.

2) I shift my focus to each inhale and exhale.

3) With my mouth closed, I inhale deeply through my nose, silently repeating a positive phrase such as "I am fearless." Instead of lifting my shoulders and forcing my chest to expand, I try to breathe from my diaphragm (the muscle just below my lungs), pulling the air in as deeply as possible, allowing it to fill my belly. I hold it for a count of five, then exhale slowly through my mouth, repeating another affirmation such as "I am loved." If mantras or phrases feel awkward to repeat, try counting, i.e., "one, two, three, four (on the inhale), five, six, seven, eight (on the exhale)."

4) If your brain needs focus, picture yourself in a peaceful setting. It could be a place you've been before (a lakeside cabin), or somewhere you've dreamed of being (your own private island). Try to fully imagine it, and involve all five senses:
- What are you seeing? (ocean, mountains, forest, etc.)
- What are you feeling? (breeze, sun warmth, rain, etc.)
- What are you hearing? (birds chirping, leaves rustling, waves hitting the beach, etc.)
- What are you smelling? (flowers, herbs, beach air, pine trees, etc.)

5) Use your five minutes to experience all sensations, while relaxing into your chosen atmosphere. After your five minutes are over, take extra time to enjoy the peace and relaxation. As you slowly stretch and open your eyes, take your calm with you.

The first two minutes of conscious breathing typically feels like short breaths, the last three or more, like long, deep, delicious breaths. To ensure that you are breathing properly, place one hand on your stomach. You should feel your belly expand slightly as you inhale, and contract as you exhale.

Laughter Is Breathing

This five-minute exercise is one way breathing can be used to orchestrate positive change in our lives. But there are others. One of the most effective is laughter.

Laughing is a marvelous phenomenon that loosens and relaxes tense muscles while moving air freely through the lungs. I know, I know, during traumatic times, laughing is the last thing you feel like doing. Yet it could be the best thing.

Many studies have shown the healing benefits of laughter. Obviously, there are countless physiological events which occur, but I can't imagine any more important than shaking loose the tensions that prevent us from breathing efficiently. There's a reason we use the phrase "breathe easier" to describe a release of anxiety.

I rediscovered the miracle of laughter several months after my divorce. I had been out with friends to movies and dinners numerous times and always forced myself to politely chuckle at jokes and witticisms. But forced laughter is almost worse than not laughing, since it takes such mental efforts.

One day while channel-surfing at home, I happened upon the movie *Airplane*. For some reason, Leslie Nielsen has always cracked me up. I absentmindedly started watching, thinking I could use the comfort of a silly favorite.

A few minutes into the movie, I got up to get something to drink. Walking by the mirror, as I glanced at my reflection, I noticed a bemused smile stretched across my face. It was a surprise to see myself caught in a moment of true enjoyment. I returned to the movie and threw myself into the zany antics of Nielsen. Before I knew it, I was laughing out loud, tears streaming down my face.

At the end of the movie, I felt better than I had in months. My shoulders were relaxed, my jaw unclenched, and best of all, my breathing was languid and deep. I couldn't have found a better remedy if I'd gone to the doctor. It felt affirming to accept pleasure back into my life.

Eventually, I was able to get my life, dignity, and self-confidence back on track. I firmly believe that my five-minute breathing rituals and the rediscovery of laughter helped restore my balance.

When I met Kim, her life was in serious need of oxygen and introspection. Learning to consciously breathe was the practice that restored her faith in herself.

Kim's Story

Kim's husband Robert had been a client of mine for two years. During our sessions he often talked about Kim. They had been married for six years, and I could tell that Robert adored his wife. He constantly alluded to her beauty and wit.

What he couldn't understand, and what he hoped I could clarify, were the reasons Kim was so self-conscious in her body. Robert was deeply saddened by her body discomfort. He typically showered Kim with sincere compliments and appreciation, frustrated that his gestures didn't seem to heal or even help relieve her body hatred.

He was baffled by the fact that on a recent vacation, Kim insisted on changing into her bathing suit in private, even though he had made several sexy attempts to share this ritual. Kim refused. She also refused to walk down the beach in her bathing suit, instead always frantically wrapping her body with cover-ups or towels before standing up. Kim told Robert that her worst fear was someone seeing her rear view in a bathing suit.

When I asked Robert if she had large buttocks, he quickly responded, "No. She wears a bathing suit as well as any *Sports Illustrated* model." He confessed feeling attracted to other women who carried their bodies with comfort and confidence, even though some were heavier than his svelte wife. Robert's greatest desire was for Kim to enjoy her body as much as he did. I explained that only Kim could heal Kim.

Then Kim got pregnant. Robert could only imagine how Kim's body anxiety would be affected by the reality of pregnancy. His gentle suggestions finally convinced her to make an appointment with me.

During our initial meeting, I was dumbstruck by Kim's physical beauty. Her features are long and lean; her hair, face, and style sophisticated and alluring. She was a nervous wreck when we met, admitting that she hated to exercise, and loved to eat, smoke, and drink, yet knew she needed to take better care of herself while pregnant.

Despite her natural gifts, Kim was visibly uncomfortable in her body. I asked her what she wished to gain from our sessions. She begged to learn how to relax. I learned that she was a fashion editor at a major publication, and that her high-paced life revolved around promoting impossibly perfect body images.

Kim confessed her multiple fears about having children: how it might affect her marriage to Robert, her horror at the idea of gaining weight, or "getting fat," as she put it. As I listened, I realized that Kim had never imagined pregnancy as sexy and empowering.

I described Step Seven to Kim, explaining that she would need to choose one time, each day, to commit five minutes to conscious breathing. Kim thought first thing in the morning would be best, prior to drinking her two cups of tea. I assigned her mantras, choosing "I am woman" on the inhale, followed by "I am whole and beautiful" on the exhale. She thought it sounded hokey, a little too "Helen Reddy," and was not sure if she could sit still that long, or repeat two phrases that she wasn't sure she believed. Yet she agreed to try Step Seven.

We devised a comfortable position that included sitting on a big pillow with her back against the wall. I suggested that during her first week, she practice her breathing ritual while listening to soothing, relaxing music.

The first step is to notice how you currently breathe. I told Kim to be prepared for a gasping reaction or even a yawn response that might occur while focusing on the oxygen entering and leaving her lungs. I also assured her that like most exercises, with time, her conscious breathing would become easier, leading to deep, calm, relaxing breaths.

Kim stuck to her five-minute breathing ritual for a full week, reporting back to me that she felt calmer and more in control of her anxious nerves. She shared that she listened to Joni Mitchell while breathing, music she loved in college. Although Kim had graduated twenty years earlier, college was the last time she remembered feeling relaxed. While she had initially resisted the mantra I had given her, she sheepishly admitted that it had sparked new lines of thinking. Kim was starting to question the image-oriented world she was immersed in every day, and the values and aspirations it engendered.

I was delighted to note that in only one week, Kim had made the connection that breathing helps shape one's life perspective and attitude. Kim said it would be easy to continue Step Seven.

One month into our weekly sessions, Kim began sharing stories of her breathing revelations. She shared that during her five-minute sessions, all of this "stuff" had been coming up about pregnancy and our society. Some of her observations, in no particular order, were:

- Our culture places such importance on a person's appearance. The fashion and media industries feed that obsession.
- Whatever happened to the worshipped belly, the center of birth and life?
- I think real beauty is to be unique.
- Pregnancy is physical truth.
- You can't hide the bulging, pregnant belly.
- I like the idea of flesh that screams out "Here I am."

She mentioned seeing a pregnant woman in a bikini on the beaches of Long Island. Her first reaction was to be repulsed. But then, she realized her admiration for the woman's unapologetic acknowledgment of her physical condition. Kim was beginning to feel more hopeful about her pregnancy, convinced it had everything to do with her calmer, more balanced perspective about her own physical changes.

Over the next few months, Kim's outlook continued to evolve. She realized that always striving for the ultimate stylish appearance had been so mentally ingrained in her upbringing, she had never considered "just saying no." Her parents were both in the fashion industry, it had always been assumed that she would work in the same field, and all of her friends and acquaintances were style setters. She had blindly accepted the presumptions and judgments of that world, using the same standards to measure her own worth. It was hardly surprising that despite the love and acceptance of her husband, she had never been able to accept her self. Before her baby was born, she was determined to find her own kernel of contentment.

A month later, Kim quit her job as a fashion editor, deciding to spend the remainder of her pregnancy in environments that were accepting and "real." She set up an office in her home, and began freelance editing (non-fashion).

As Kim progressed through pregnancy, adjusting to her new life away from the office, she experienced many positive changes. Most important was her newfound enjoyment of relaxing. In our weekly meetings, she excitedly shared that her five minutes of conscious breathing had grown into thirty, and she preferred silence instead of Joni Mitchell during this half-hour.

She believed that her breathing practice helped eliminate her desire for cigarettes, with each conscious breath reminding her of the health of her lungs and developing baby. Furthermore, she mentioned a new attraction toward Robert. She wasn't sure if it was due to pregnancy hormones, or her calmer state of mind, but she was thrilled to be feeling a new spark. Kim thought it was also the fact that she no longer looked at pictures of models for eight hours a day.

When I asked why that made a difference, she explained that being focused on models all day made her feel insecure, as if she never measured up. Because of the fashion industry's obsession with slenderness, which promotes female body hatred, it's hardly surprising that many women feel the same as Kim. Through Kim's daily breathing meditations, though, she was able—for a few precious moments—to escape the impossible body images and standards constantly bombarding us from the media.

I thought that Kim was ready to take her body acceptance to a new level. I suggested that once a week, she do her five-minute breathing ritual in the nude. Even with her newfound "enlightenment," and her belief that "pregnancy is physical truth," this was a tall order. She simply couldn't, she said. Not now anyway. I left it at that. No *Feel Good Naked* exercise should ever be forced.

What was wonderful to observe was Robert's and Kim's renewed passion for each other. During my sessions with Robert, he would virtually glow at the mention of Kim, thanking me profusely for whatever I was doing. I reminded him that it was what Kim was doing, not me.

Seven months later, Kim and Robert had Lilly, a healthy baby girl.

Kim was amazed at how much she actually enjoyed the entire birthing process. She gained forty pounds during pregnancy. While the old Kim would have rushed into a crash diet to lose the weight as quickly as possible, the new Kim asked if we could continue working together to sensibly shed the weight.

As our weekly meetings turned into cardiovascular jaunts around Central Park, Kim talked about how she hoped to raise Lilly. She mentioned countless times her desire to not pass on the many body hang-ups she had growing up. That she hoped to raise a woman who measured her self-worth through her truest accomplishments, not her dress size.

It is now several years later. Kim continues to breathe consciously for five to thirty minutes each day. She wakes up earlier than Robert and Lilly, if that's the only quiet time she'll have. She has no desire to ever smoke again, finally feeling a peaceful balance between her mind, body, and spirit. Kim trusts her internal confidence, which is reflected in her outward beauty that she now owns.

To my delight, a year after the birth of Lilly, Kim tried the exercise I had suggested while she was pregnant: doing her five-minute breathing ritual in the nude. It was not as traumatic as she feared; in fact, she found it enjoyable. It's not part of her regular routine, but she does it every now and then, to remind herself "that naked is beautiful."

As for Robert, he couldn't wait to tell me that on their family trip to Club Med, Kim ran around the beach in a bikini without a wrap, chasing after their daughter; she also willingly shared a bath with him one night, after Lilly was fast asleep. He was shocked and overjoyed with her serene body confidence, feeling that it has added a wonderful new dimension to their marriage.

Summary:

Conscious breathing can bring calm to chaos, peace to anxiety, insight to confusion. Deep, effective breathing can be accomplished many ways; two of my favorites are five-minute conscious breathing rituals and laughter.

Develop your own style and method for conscious breathing, making sure you do it for at least five minutes. I like to sit on my bed, back to the wall, legs crossed, hands on knees. I repeat affirmative phrases as I inhale deeply through my nose, and exhale through my mouth. You can also count forward and backward, or if you need a focus, imagine a relaxing setting and conjure up the sensations you would experience if you were there. If you're brave, try it naked.

Through conscious breathing, Kim discovered insights she'd never previously had time for. For example, she realized she had been immersed in a career that promotes female insecurity. It wasn't until she became pregnant and left the fashion industry that she realized the price of looking at pictures of models all day. Her occupation had fueled her body hatred, and the effects were spilling into her marriage. As well, her constant self-doubt had created a nervousness that promoted many unhealthy habits, such as smoking.

Step Seven taught Kim how to breathe consciously while taking an honest self-inventory. Her daily five-minute sessions helped sort out what was—and wasn't—important as she approached parenthood. She was able to make important changes that brought her life more closely in line with her true values, before her daughter was born.

As you make Step Seven part of your *Feel Good Naked* lifestyle, remember that it will become a habit that your body and mind enjoy—a wonderful, rejuvenating, calming ritual that will serve you as well in extraordinary circumstances as it does in ordinary ones.

STEP **8**

TAKE 30 MINUTES OF PRIVATE TIME EACH DAY.

A Thirty-Minute Investment that Will Ultimately Save You Time

There is a popular phrase going around these days, often attributed to John Lennon, which seems to define middle-class life in the twenty-first century: "Life is what happens while you're making other plans."

It's easy to hear this acknowledgment of our schedule-driven existence and chuckle. But for most of us, it hits dangerously close to home.

Are you:

- stressed out
- unproductive
- out of time
- constantly exhausted and nervous?

Is a half-hour of private time as difficult for you to imagine as a month off from all responsibilities? Welcome to the ranks of the overstressed and time-challenged. In short, your life is out of balance. As much as you would like to add more hours to your day, it's a futile wish. As many as twenty million Americans suffer from stress-related illnesses. Countless studies have proven that stress and anxiety play a role in health problems, ranging from the common cold to cancer. In fact, it's estimated that half the patients seen by doctors are there because of stress-related symptoms. In addition to the health risks, these emotions are detrimental to body, mind, and spirit, ultimately sabotaging personal levels of happiness and productivity.

Whatever happened to the concept of spending a day going where the wind blows, a weekend relaxing, or a vacation without an agenda? Those "luxuries" flew out the back door the same time kids, promotions, and the trappings of modern life walked in the front door. The fact is, without ample down time, our awake time becomes less fruitful. We're never really parked, or running on all cylinders.

While the average woman tries desperately to manage a career and/or a home with some semblance of a personal life, private "alone" time, like exercise time, gets pushed aside. You may not even have "alone" time when brushing your teeth. But in order to create a symbiotic relationship between body and mind, you must feed both. Private time is one of the greatest sources of mind-body nourishment, and contrary to what you may believe, it doesn't require making huge adjustments in your life. The thirty minutes you set aside often winds up creating an extra half-hour in the day, thanks to a clearer mind, more focused energy, and better efficiency. You might be shocked at how well the world gets along without thirty minutes of your attention every day.

Still convinced you can't possibly afford to spare thirty minutes? Ask yourself if you would find the time if your mother called and urgently needed your help, your child's fever required an unexpected trip to the doctor, or your computer crashed and you had to spend thirty extra minutes re-entering data. Even though you would never plan for those things, you would find time if they arose. We all make time for things we consider important. And what could be more important than your sanity?

Think about your average day. Even the busiest person steals a few unsatisfying minutes of daydreaming—a quick zone out—nothing that really rejuvenates, yet still adds up to thirty minutes. Imagine if you used that half-hour to "buy" productivity for the rest of your day. Remember, don't think of it as "wasted" time; consider it as "recharging your batteries," which ultimately enables you to accomplish more than you would otherwise.

Once you decide to try Step Eight, keep in mind that your half-hour can be spent any way you choose. It can be a time to meditate, breathe consciously (integrated with Step Seven), or to exercise, if the ten minutes in Step Three is not enough. Other suggestions include soaking in a hot bubble bath, reading a book, writing in a journal, collecting your thoughts over a cup of tea, drawing, listening to music, napping, or praying. The best part is, you get to decide. The only rules are that you do it alone, choosing options that feed your spirit and relax your mind.

Create Your Own Ashram

Rather than getting stressed out about being stressed, the key is doing something constructive to help your body and mind process stress. Even having all the luxuries, freedom, and love we could ever imagine would create its own type of stress. But we can reduce the factors that contribute to stress. And we can cultivate the kind of balanced, contented lives that take daily stress in stride, refusing to allow ourselves to internalize or catastrophize ordinary worries.

Step Eight is a great place to start. We hear so much about spending "quality time" with those we love. Step Eight is about spending "quality time" with ourselves. It's a thirty-minute respite from the onslaught of things over which we have no control: phones, appointments, milk spills, inflation worries. Think of this half-hour as your own personal island, where you get to decide everything. Later in this chapter I will discuss spending this time being active. However, if you are like me and choose to spend this ritual being still and quiet, I want to help you create a spa-like environment for your getaway.

It's important to create a personal space where you remove all unnecessary clutter, surrounding yourself with favorite relaxing sounds, smells, sights, and textures. It can be inside (a spare room or corner) or outside (a hot tub or garden area). Candles, incense, calming music, waterscapes, scented oils, and a cozy, comfortable place to sit will help shift your state of mind. As you enter your space, take off your shoes, and be especially conscious of how you feel. Give yourself permission to relax in your sanctuary.

I begin my thirty minutes by incorporating Step Seven—conscious breathing. This helps accelerate my relaxation process. I generally choose early mornings for this ritual, using the time to visualize daily goals. I don't always meditate for a full half-hour. Sometimes I write. Occasionally I read. But I always insist that whatever I do feed my spirit and relax my mind (no shopping lists or checkbook balancing). After thirty minutes, I feel renewed, empowered, and amply prepared for the new day. Frankly, I credit Steps Seven and Eight for guiding me calmly through the challenges of successfully balancing marriage and parenting with my career.

Many of my clients have also found mornings to be the best time for this half-hour of serenity. Early morning offers a stillness that quickly evaporates once the day kicks into high gear. If you have children, it may be the only time, before they awake, that your house is perfectly quiet.

Nocturnal Pleasure

If you are not a morning person, early hours will not be your best time to mentally refresh and nourish. Instead, spend your thirty minutes alone at night, before going to sleep. This can be a wonderful time to review your day and quiet your mind. I highly recommend a relaxing warm bubble bath that's been infused with scented bath salts. Or, sneak off to your personal sanctuary, put on a favorite CD, lie on a floor mat, close your eyes, and visualize each body part, starting with your toes and slowly moving up to your head, melting into a relaxed state.

Other great ways to relax at night are:

- applying a face mask
- putting a velvety eye balm on closed eyes
- soaking your feet in warm scented water
- surrounding your bubble bath with lit candles
- placing an eye pillow over your closed eyes

Thirty Minutes on the Go

You may choose to spend Step Eight being physical.

Thirty minutes of exercise offers many mind-body advantages, while being one of the most effective anti-aging weapons available. As we discussed in Step Three, you don't have to engage in lengthy workouts to reap innumerable wellness benefits. And even if you choose to "get physical" during your private time, it doesn't have to be an aerobic activity. You might enjoy anaerobic strength training or resistance training, or spending your time stretching while increasing your flexibility. If your half-hour is going to be active, here are my favorite suggestions:

Walking: Whenever I call my father and say I am feeling blocked, stressed, or anxious, he always says, "Go take a walk." I recommend his wise advice to everyone. Walking is one of the most effective ways to reduce mental and emotional "noise." It's also a wonderful, healthy way to be with yourself, and is excellent for developing a new outlook—literally and figuratively—

while enhancing your cardiovascular system. It doesn't have to be intense to be beneficial. Walking helps reduce stress, depression, mood swings, and water retention.

Resistance Training: If you choose to develop muscular strength during your half-hour, alternate your training with stretching. My suggestion is to strength train Monday, Wednesday, and Friday, while stretching Tuesday, Thursday, Saturday, and Sunday. You can combat loss of bone mass and muscle strength with resistance training. Lifting appropriately weighted dumbbells several times a week can do more for your bones than medication. It's never too late to build bone density, or to learn how to do bicep curls, squats, crunches, lateral raises, pliés, lunges, or push-ups. A good book for women who wish to learn basic strength-training exercises is *Fat to Firm at Any Age* by Alisa Bauman, Sari Harrar, and the editors of Prevention Health Books.

Stretching: Because muscles, tendons, and ligaments tighten as you age, stretching is both a relaxing and therapeutic way to spend your thirty minutes. Stretching will help loosen and relax your limbs, while reducing your risk of injury and calming your mind. Stretching is my favorite part of yoga or Pilates exercises. It is an extremely effective way to relax while improving your body.

Tick, Tick, Boom

We all know people who, like the white rabbit in *Alice in Wonderland*, seem to constantly be racing to catch up with themselves, alternating between states of panic, worry, agitation, and martyrdom. We may be shocked to occasionally catch a glimpse of that person in the mirror—as we rush from one commitment to another. But, as my client Julie found, no one is so important, so crucial, so essential to the world that they cannot find thirty minutes for themselves each day. In fact, taking this time may actually enhance the progress of the world—or at least our perception of it.

Julie's Story

Julie and her husband Don agreed that he would stay home while they raise their two small daughters. Julie is a successful gynecologist. I met Julie while having my annual check-up with her associate. When her partner found out what I did for a living, she insisted that I meet Julie, who had voiced her interest in hiring someone to help her "get her old body back."

In less than two minutes, which was all Julie had, we pulled out our appointment books and agreed to meet at 5:00 P.M. at the end of the week, where she miraculously had an opening in her schedule. She explained that she might need to cancel if an emergency arose. I walked away telling her to make herself the emergency. She looked at me wistfully and chuckled.

Julie and I met as planned. Her main goal was to lose weight. She had gained fifty pounds with her last pregnancy and had only lost ten of the fifty pounds since her daughter was born three years ago. She explained how uncomfortable she felt being overweight, knowing the medical health risks caused by excess weight. She felt both scared of the consequences she was courting and unable to do anything to avoid them.

I asked Julie if her weight was the only issue troubling her. She laughed and blurted out something like, "Yes, unless you've discovered a way to add about three more hours to the day."

Julie admitted that for the past year, her life had become intolerably busy—and unbalanced. Her medical practice had lost two doctors who had not been replaced, shifting an inordinate amount of work onto the remaining physicians. Ten- to twelve-hour work days had become Julie's norm. In addition to her work stress, she also felt compelled to carry a demanding load at home. While Don handled many of the household duties, Julie habitually prepared meals for her family. It wasn't that her husband wasn't willing to take the cooking tasks, but that Julie had "always done it." I could tell that Julie was a self-possessed woman, one who rarely admitted needing help.

I asked her to describe her typical day. It included:

- waking up at 5:30 A.M.
- making breakfast for Don and her children
- leaving for work by 7 A.M.
- seeing patients from 7:30 A.M. until 6 P.M. (with a brief lunch squeezed in)
- arriving home by 7 P.M.
- helping prepare dinner and eating with her family
- reading to her children and putting them asleep at 8:30 P.M.
- reviewing her day's paperwork
- passing out at 10 P.M.

When I sympathized that her schedule sounded like a real backbreaker, I saw tears welling up in Julie's eyes. She apologized, saying she'd been under a lot of stress lately, feeling totally "out of control" in her personal life. "At the office I'm fine," she shared, "maybe because I have to be since people's lives depend on my competency. But at home, I don't have any relief, or relaxation time. My husband is with the girls all day, so I feel it's only fair to take over when I'm home. And I want to be with them. Yet there's nothing left over for me." Julie said she felt "out of whack"— emotionally, physically, socially, and spiritually. She mentioned that medical school and residency seemed easier than her current life—which was saying a lot. Her life had become impossible to manage, with no time for meaningful rewards.

My immediate thought was that Julie needed space in her schedule for herself. Her batteries were out of juice. When her children were born, healthy eating habits had gone by the wayside, but her weight was a symptom of a bigger problem. Julie was a physician who took excellent care of everyone but herself. She desperately needed time in her life to be, rather than do.

Many women I've met share the same emotional pattern. They go, go, go, making sure everyone else is taken care of and catered to, telling themselves they'll attend to their needs "later." But "later" never comes, and resentment grows, manifesting itself in little ways. Perhaps they develop a slight martyr complex, or habitually eat "treats" they feel they deserve. But eventually the martyrdom becomes obvious to others, and the "treats" start taking their toll, either in weight gain if the treats are food-related, or financially if the woman tries to relieve her unhappiness through shopping.

I firmly believed that if Julie could incorporate Step Eight into her life, she would begin to feel more nurtured, which would give her the serenity to manage her weight and her overbooked life more successfully.

By her dubious demeanor, I think Julie thought I was going to ask her to buy a treadmill and wake up even earlier than she already did to use it. Instead, I asked her where she felt most relaxed in her home. She was taken aback, but after thinking for a moment, told me her study was her only real haven. I suggested she set up a space in her study where she could sit quietly, close her eyes, and relax for thirty minutes each day.

Her reaction was priceless. She started laughing and said, "No, really, what do you want me to do?" I told Julie that her weight gain was symptomatic of her out-of-control life; until she took hold of her life, she couldn't take hold of the process of losing weight. This gave her pause. She thought she had hired a fitness therapist, and here I was, telling her to find time to relax each day for thirty minutes. I asked if I could suggest ideas for setting up this special place. We agreed to meet that weekend at her home so I could observe her study, making suggestions for converting the space into a personal zone.

I didn't so much visit Julie and her family that weekend, I experienced them. The sensory levels in her house were overwhelming. The kids were running through each room whooping and yelling, Don was watching television with the volume turned up, and there was a radio playing loudly somewhere else in the house. When we entered her study, there were so many books and magazine stacks, we could barely find room for both of us to sit down. Once we settled in, I felt quite clear about how to guide Julie toward a more peaceful set-up.

We shut the door to the hubbub downstairs, and I had her close her eyes, make herself comfortable, and take several deep breaths. I laid both hands on her shoulders and repeated the phrase, "Relax and release." Once she seemed to calm down, I asked her to name her favorite smell (jasmine) and her favorite music (Sinatra).

I quietly repeated the phrase, "relax and release," while Julie sat still and breathed deeply. Several times she asked how long it had been, and I suggested she forget the time, allowing herself to decompress for a full thirty minutes.

When I guided Julie to open her eyes, her entire countenance had undergone a transformation. She had a wonderful, serene glow and a contented smile. "Wow," she effused, "what hit me?" I explained that she had successfully experienced Step Eight and that I wanted her to tell me when she could commit to this same practice each day. She felt the best time would be in the early morning, but she was reluctant to get up any earlier than her current 5:30 A.M.

I noted that currently she was making breakfast for everyone—could her husband take on that responsibility to free up thirty minutes? I could tell she was reluctant, but when pressed, she couldn't give any good reason not to ask. I mentioned that in order to help herself she was going to have to get more aggressive about asking others for help. I reassured her there was no shame in admitting she needed help to balance her life. In fact, it's surprising how sympathetically most people respond when we admit we can't do it alone.

In addition, I suggested that Julie purchase either jasmine incense or a jasmine candle to light during her personal time, while softly playing a favorite Sinatra CD. I recommended that she remove the clutter from her study, throwing out all magazines she had not read in the last six months. Energized by her refreshing interlude, Julie decided she would clean out her study that afternoon, excited to create a more soothing environment.

Julie and I agreed to speak on the telephone one week later to see how she was doing.

When we talked, there was noticeable spunk in Julie's voice.

She commented on the immense changes in her energy levels and attitude since spending thirty minutes alone each day. Julie noted that people at work had asked her what she had been doing, commenting that she looked different. She was thrilled to relate that she had cleared out the clutter in her study, purchased a jasmine candle, a special pillow to sit on, and a new Sinatra compilation CD.

For the first week, Julie had spent her time simply meditating. It had been so long since she'd had time to relax, let alone reflect, she was reveling in the opportunity. I told her she was free to do whatever she wanted during her personal time: read, write, or engage in another rewarding activity.

One month later, Julie called with exciting news. "I don't know how it happened, but I've lost five pounds," she exclaimed. As we went through her daily routine, she revealed subtle yet profound changes in her eating habits. Since relinquishing breakfast duties to Don, who was happy to assume them, she had been enjoying more variety and nutrition in her first meal of the day. Before, her choices had always been quick, sugar-laden toaster pastries or sweet cereals her daughters liked. Now, Don enjoyed preparing healthy meals that often included fresh fruit, yogurt, eggs, granola, or an occasional breakfast meat. Their daughters quickly acclimated to the new menus, and Julie found that by eating a healthy breakfast, she was no longer loading up on mid-morning snacks. Between her personal renewal time each morning, and a healthy, hearty breakfast, she started each day "ready to take on the world, instead of ready to go back to bed."

On my recommendation, Julie began leaving her office for her lunch break. Before, when she ate at her desk, she would run down to the deli, grab the special of the day, paying little attention to how large the portions were or what exactly she was eating, race back to her office, and wolf it down. Now, she used five minutes in the morning to pack a healthy sandwich, some raw veggies, yogurt, and a piece of fruit. There was a conference room in her office that was rarely used; it became her noontime refuge.

Julie was thrilled with her mental and physical progress, and wondered about incorporating more exercise into either her morning ritual or her noontime break. She didn't want to lose the calming benefits of meditating, but was eager to expedite her weight loss. I suggested a combination of both: taking a brisk walk during her weekly personal time on Tuesdays and Thursdays, while spending the rest of her personal time in her sanctuary. I told Julie that after fulfilling this schedule for two months, if she still wanted to add more exercise, she could walk on Mondays and Fridays.

Once Julie lost ten pounds, I added a *Feel Good Naked* assignment. Knowing her study had a good lock on the door, I asked her to spend at least one day a week sketching herself in the nude. I knew Julie had taken some drawing classes, and enjoyed the focus and creativity of freehand sketching. Like most clients, when I suggest doing anything naked, she was reluctant, afraid her daughters would barge in. I reminded her of the lock, and her daughters' respect for her private time, and she acknowledged that she was really embarrassed. Gradually, she warmed to the idea, recognizing the value of getting to know the body she felt had betrayed her over the past few years. Not only did Julie end up enjoying this ritual, it renewed her interest in drawing, encouraging her to use more of her personal time in this creative pursuit.

Six months after we began working together, Julie had lost twenty pounds and was as close to being a new woman as anyone I have worked with. In addition to being twenty pounds away from her pre-pregnancy weight, she had become more assertive in other areas of her life as well. Within a few months, the staff was back to full strength, and she was able to cut her work week back to a manageable thirty-five hours. Seeing what a great job her husband did on breakfasts, Julie began sharing dinner duties with him as well, asking for help whenever she saw a frantic day on the horizon. Knowing how hard it was for Julie to ask for assistance, Don was happy to jump in.

By taking the time to nurture and honor herself for thirty minutes every day, Julie no longer lived the frenzied, sacrificing life of the martyr—and she no longer needed the stolen moments and unhealthy "treats" over-committed women usually give themselves to feel whole. Instead, she discovered the paradox of Step Eight: instead of diminishing our already limited hours each day, thirty minutes of personal renewal time adds clarity, focus, energy, productivity, and purpose to each day.

Summary:

Like many women, Julie believed she could juggle the demands of a high-stress career with the demands of motherhood and marriage. She wanted to do all three perfectly, and was forgetting someone in the process: herself. Julie had run out of gas and desperately needed to recharge her batteries. Step Eight taught Julie how to give herself the gift she gave everyone else so readily: the gift of time. In the process, she let go of her martyr complex and the need to fulfill herself with unnecessary tasks and quick snacking.

Once Julie began honoring herself with thirty minutes of private time, she also began to notice a big change in her body. By delegating the breakfast chores to her husband, she benefited from healthier meal choices. She also stopped unconsciously inhaling her lunches at her desk. By adding exercise to her life, Julie was able to burn calories, lose weight, and minimize her high stress level. Julie found a combination of personal time and exercise to be the perfect solution for helping her body, while also clearing her mind and nurturing her spirit.

Use these thirty minutes any way you choose. It can be relaxation based or exercise related. Whether you wake up at 5:30 A.M. or sneak off to the bath after everyone is asleep, carve out this half-hour and stick to it religiously. You will find that contrary to a time "expense," it's an "investment" that will pay untold dividends.

STEP 9

WRITE YOURSELF A LOVE LETTER ONCE A MONTH.

Mirror, Mirror . . .

Did you know that:

- Marilyn Monroe wore a size fourteen?
- If Barbie were a real woman, she'd have to walk on all fours due to her proportions?
- A recent psychological study found that three minutes spent looking at models in a fashion magazine caused 70 percent of women readers to feel depressed, guilty, and shameful? (Just ask Kim from Step Seven.)
- On any given day, almost half of all American women are on a diet?

As shocking as these factoids are, what's even more staggering is what they say about our female state of mind—how our perceptions about the female body, whether positive or negative, are so warped, we've backed ourselves into a harsh corner of expectation and judgment. And the target we set our sights on most? Ourselves.

It's not just the average woman who buys into this self-directed negativity. By looking at the expressions and body language of celebrities, whether it's in person, in a magazine, or on television, I can immediately tell how they feel about being naked.

The sad thing is, as the *Feel Good Naked* program teaches, happiness and contentment are not nearly as dependent on a perfect body as we're led to believe. Think about all the people—famous or not—who embody the textbook definition of leanness, yet lead troubled, even destructive lives. As devoted as we are to a "think thin" mentality, skinny is obviously not a magic pill for happiness.

What's more, this criticism is not only limited to our own physical qualities. As women, we are amazingly quick to pass judgment on others, as well.

This was evident to me at the beginning of my fitness career. I was working with a single woman in her late thirties. She had just found herself on the receiving end of a traumatic break-up. One day she was late to our session, which was out of character. She arrived breathless, apologizing. I could see she had been crying. "I've been going through all of his old love letters," she choked. "Oh, no," I moaned, "why torture yourself that way?" "Because he says such wonderful things about me," she replied. "Even though I'm dying over losing him, there's something about seeing compliments written down that makes me believe them." A light went on in my head. For this poor woman, feeling good about herself wasn't possible without the affirmation coming from someone else. Even though the source of the compliments was highly suspect, his letters were better than nothing; certainly more credible than trying to convince herself of her worthwhile attributes.

This episode exemplified how brainwashed and passive we've become when measuring and determining our self-worth. How can it be that the (supposedly) most progressive, self-aware, self-actualized people are willing to let others tell us what to think of ourselves? Yet something good came out of the experience. I learned the importance of written words to help us discover and believe in our individual strengths.

Step Nine is designed to help you recognize what you like about you—then convince yourself of it. At the risk of sounding like someone from a relationship infomercial, this step promotes self-love, which ultimately leads to embracing your unique goodness from the inside out.

Dear Me

When I ask a client to write a love letter to herself, the response is always entertaining. Some people balk, laugh, or get very nervous. I don't think I've ever had anyone say, "Hey, great idea. I'm going home to do that right now." In fact, what generally happens, if I can get them to try, is they sit down to write and nothing comes out.

Sometimes, just to break their mental block, I have clients write a hate letter to themselves. That's right—a hate letter. I have them write down all the things they don't like. Sadly, this always comes easier. But once all their negative opinions are down on paper, I tell them, "Okay, since you've acknowledged the ways you aren't perfect, now you can let them go." And I have them burn the letter. Once they've let go of the negatives, I say, "There must be some positives left over." And I send them off to try the love letter again.

Let me be the first to say that a love letter to yourself is difficult to write. But it is tremendously valuable in making the transition from self-hatred to self-love. It's especially valuable for single people or people who are stuck in unhappy relationships. We all deserve to be recognized for our individual strengths—both those that the universe and our parents have given us, and those that we have earned. Of course, it's wonderful if the recognition comes from others. But it's not necessary. Ironically, self-written love letters fuel self-respect, which in essence reflects the way you present yourself to the world. Self-respect will dramatically improve the way others see and treat you.

So, where do you start? I hope you're not someone who can't think of a single positive quality about yourself to put down on paper. But if you are, go ahead and try the hate letter exercise first. It will help vanquish the demons and "tapes" that continue playing in your head about your character or body defects. Done? Now that you've acknowledged those shortcomings—they don't need to keep hanging around in your psyche. It's like saying to that little voice in your head, "Okay, I've heard you. You can leave now."

Now, start your love letter. I recommend writing a true letter, beginning with "Dear (your name)", as if you were writing a friend. Next, it's time to have an "out-of-body" experience, to detach and imagine yourself as you appear to the outside world. It may be helpful to look at yourself in the mirror, to see yourself as others see you. Most people find it's not as difficult as it is disorienting. But it's where you need to be for this exercise— looking at yourself from a new, more objective perspective.

Once you've adopted this detached viewpoint, think back to your last interaction with another person, imagining how you were perceived. It can be a phone call or a face-to-face conversation. Replay the conversation in your mind. What felt right? Hone in on the smallest things you did right. Were you courteous? Did you smile? Were you kind? Patient? Succinct? Articulate? Resourceful? Do not use this memory to rake yourself over the coals for things that didn't go right. Instead, write down, "I want to compliment you on your conversation with (name of other person). Sure, it didn't go perfectly, and there were some things you'd say differently next time. But you were . . . (here, list the positive adjectives that describe your part of the conversation) . . . Good job." Maybe you have only one positive memory—that's okay, write it down.

Silly? A waste of time? No. This exercise is a step toward overcoming the discomfort of "bragging" about yourself. Few people are willing to flatter themselves with sweeping accolades like "generous," "loyal," or "loving."

At least, not initially. But by using a specific—if trivial—incident as a starting place, most of us are willing to recognize particular examples where we did certain things right. The good news is, if we did it right at least once, we probably do it right at other times also.

This simple reflection may be all that comprises your first letter. If it feels right, just sign your letter "Love, (your name) or "Your Secret Admirer." If the memory of your last successful exchange has warmed you up and you're willing to describe other virtues, continue on. Most important is to list your character virtues first, but if you're feeling especially empowered, you can also expand your compliments to include physical attributes as well. Your letter can be whatever length feels comfortable. I advise clients to keep their letters relatively short; you'll have more opportunities to write letters, so you don't have to include every good quality in this one.

When you've completed your letter, place it in an envelope addressed to yourself, and mail it. That's right, put a stamp on it, and send it off. Won't you feel silly mailing a letter to yourself? Maybe. Who cares? It's a free country, and really, aren't you tired of coming home to only junk mail anyway?

When you receive your letter in the mail, don't open it with the rest of the bills and flyers. Take it to a private place (perhaps incorporate it into your thirty minutes of private time, Step Eight). Carefully open and read it, as if you had received the mail unexpectedly from a treasured friend or relative. Let the words sink in. Close your eyes and take a deep cleansing breath, knowing there's at least one person (and likely many others) in the world who appreciates and recognizes your unique set of virtues.

Once you're ready to move on to physical attributes, write your love letter naked. If you'd like, incorporate a small compact mirror to help you focus on individual features. Sure, you may not be wild about the skin that droops underneath your upper arm. But wow, what a sexy shoulder. Ignore the crow's feet, and concentrate on the beautiful color of your eyes. Repeat this simple exercise once a month. It's a wonderful ritual of empowerment and self-renewal.

The Three Most Important Opinions: Those of Me, Myself, and I

Central to the theme of this chapter—and a recurring topic throughout the *Feel Good Naked* program—is the idea of giving yourself both permission and power to stand in awe of yourself. To honor your strengths, your individual needs, and your personal paths of discovery and growth.

With this in mind, I want to return to the story that opened this chapter, about the woman who had been unceremoniously dumped by her boyfriend. Hers was not a particularly unusual circumstance, but what was especially sad was that her entire self-worth was dependent on the actions and opinions of someone else. This is one of the most pervasive and harmful dysfunctions we as a society typically accept and even promote. It doesn't have to be a boyfriend. Remember Erin from Step One, and Jennifer from Step Three, whose self-views were seriously interwoven with the approval of their mothers? If we are ever to live truly happy, balanced, fulfilled lives, we must learn to draw pride and contentment from our personal inventory.

Relying on a man, or a relationship, to provide you with self-confidence only sets you up for failure when you are not in a relationship. And trust me—whether due to break-up, death, or other circumstances, chances are there will be a time when you're not in a relationship. Why relinquish the one miraculous gift we can give ourselves—our personal power?

It was not until I found myself single in my thirties that I understood the profound power of this step. Through the hard-earned lessons I've shared throughout this book, I eventually learned that the greatest lessons about life and love were inside of myself. As clichéd as it sounds, it was only after becoming thoroughly comfortable with myself that I was able to find happiness with another person.

Many of the things that we associate sharing with a mate, such as eating great food, enjoying an outdoor activity, going to a play or movie, listening to live music, or even receiving a love letter, do not actually require a partner. When you go out by yourself, no one is nearly as focused on the fact that you're alone as you are. Remember—most people have plenty to worry about in their own lives without wondering what you're up to. An interesting exercise is to compare your self-consciousness when you are alone at an event, to when you are alone but waiting for someone to meet you. When you are meeting someone, you probably feel little discomfort that you are alone, since you know someone will be joining you shortly. Contrast this to how you feel when you know you are alone for the duration—embarrassed and worried that others are thinking you're "weird." The fact is, to those around you—there is no way to tell the difference. You look exactly the same whether you're waiting for someone or going solo. The difference is your perception.

In each of my steps I've tried to suggest small but powerful actions that will help you find new sources of personal strength. A deep, nourishing spring of affirmations have been there all along, waiting to be tapped. These reserves are inside of you and are available twenty-four hours a day, seven days a week, for the rest of your life. You don't have to rely on lovers or parents or bosses or children or anyone. It's your core, your essence—you, stripped down to the essentials. You, naked.

By sitting down each month and writing yourself a love letter, you will eventually understand the impact of this exercise on your self-confidence. By recording a few sentences that reinforce your integrity and dignity, you will be invoking the power of the written word. It's right there on paper—it must be true. Eventually, you will begin to like who you are. Of course, no one is always 100 percent happy. But giving your own voice precedence over the blaring, unhealthy proclamations of others, including the media, can be one of the most liberating events of your—or any woman's—life.

Vu is a wonderful example of the power of Step Nine.

Vu's Story

Vu was thirty years old, pursuing a career in advertising when we met. She was married to Jay, a hugely successful entrepreneur who oversaw several different companies. They lived an exciting life that included lots of travel and fun—from sailing in exotic seas, to ritzy "society" dinners, to the usual luxury toys and trappings of wealth. Vu told me that she liked their life the way it was, but Jay was pressuring her to have children. He came from a big family and wanted the same for himself and Vu. She had also come from a big family—but unlike Jay, had little interest in creating one. She shared her theory that when you have more than two people in a family, "someone gets the short end of the stick."

At our first meeting, one of the first things Vu told me was that Jay was surrounded by attractive women at work who were mostly in their twenties. She admitted feeling threatened and less beautiful than all of them, yet hoped that if we worked together, she could "beat them out" with a better body. I thought her choice of words was interesting. Vu is a small-framed, Asian woman whom I thought had a great body with beautiful refined features.

Unlike most career women, Vu was willing to commit as many as six hours a week to her physical goals. We began meeting at the gym at 5:30 A.M. three mornings a week. She wanted her body to look like Jennifer Lopez's—with more muscle and less fat—even though her body didn't carry much fat to begin with. She constantly complained about her life, body, and husband while she exercised. I soon realized her work needed to be more about self-love, and less about push-ups. I hoped our training sessions might eventually lead her to the cathartic realization of her abysmal lack of self-acceptance.

Vu reminded me of other women I have met and worked with. She had a successful career, a loving husband, a great house, many friends, lots of money and the luxuries and adventures it can buy. But as much as she claimed to enjoy her lifestyle, it was clear she was miserable in her life. Most of her complaints were about Jay . . . he never did enough for her. In fact, no one ever did enough for Vu.

Then Vu got pregnant. She mentioned it to me matter-of-factly, with the quick addition, "But I'm not going to let it change our life." I just smiled patiently. Even though I was childless at the time, I knew the unlikeliness of that declaration coming true.

Jay suggested that Vu quit her job, which had been a focus of her ire the past few months. She jumped at the opportunity. I got the sense, however, that her reason for quitting was not because she had been dissatisfied with her career, but because Jay "owed it to her." She had often made snide remarks about how little he did around the house, how everything was left to her.

During her pregnancy, Vu and I altered the intensity of our workouts, but we continued to meet three times each week. After her son was born, we quickly resumed our workouts.

I was shocked at Vu's continued negativity, thinking that the birth of her baby would show her the brighter side of life. Instead, she complained about life with an infant. She didn't like anything about being a new mother. She hated the breast-feeding, bathing her baby, dressing her baby, being with her baby. She was still miserable. And—surprise, surprise—having a newborn around was not only changing Vu's life, it was turning her life upside down. When I asked about Jay, she mentioned (with no appreciation) that he had gladly taken the night shift formula feedings and that he seemed to be in love with the baby. She also mentioned, rolling her eyes, that Jay wanted more children.

Vu trained her body rigorously and was quickly back in pre-pregnancy shape. The one thing in her life that seemed to give her satisfaction was fitting into the same sized jeans she had worn in college.

Given her attitude toward her first child, I was frankly shocked when Vu proceeded to have two more children—both daughters—in quick succession. She claimed Jay was pressuring her, and while she griped mightily about his shortcomings, I also knew how much she feared losing his love and attention. Adding to the family did little to improve Vu's attitude about motherhood. After the birth of their second child, Vu and Jay hired a nanny to help with the children. Yet she still admitted she couldn't wait until her children were older and less demanding. Vu seemed deeply unhappy with the roles of mother, wife, and woman. But whenever I probed these subjects, she reacted quickly and defensively, as if an open wound had been touched.

It was interesting to me how Vu presented herself to the world. Appearances were everything to her. She was always neat, stylish, and accessorized. She tried to temper her sharp, strident nature with a witty, sophisticated, world-weary attitude. Her outward demeanor did not fool me. I saw a woman who was deeply insecure, ungrateful for her privileged lifestyle, unappreciative of her husband and children, and in serious denial about the unhappiness inside of her.

At this point I had been working with Vu for five years. She had attained the body of her dreams, yet she wasn't any closer to feeling good naked. She was not interested in practicing the *Feel Good Naked* steps that didn't relate to her physical appearance. I was losing hope that I would ever be able to help her heal.

And then, bam—Vu's worst fear became reality. Jay left her for another woman. After nine years together, he had reached his limit with her, and frankly, I was reaching mine.

Jay had come home from work, asked Vu to sit down, and proceeded to tell her he had fallen in love with Diana, a co-worker. It had been Jay's beautiful co-workers who had originally driven Vu to seek my help. But, in an ironic twist of fate, the woman he had fallen in love with was not one of the beauties. Diana was an average-looking, pleasantly plump woman, actually slightly older than Jay. But she had been a patient, kind confidante and friend over the past few years—something Vu certainly wasn't. He told Vu bluntly that he could no longer live with her dismal attitude about life and raising children.

Initially, Vu was more stunned than anything else. I don't know which bewildered her more: the fact that Jay had fallen in love with someone else, or the reality that the other woman was, by societal standards, so much less "desirable." She could not get over how she had misperceived what was important to him. Although Vu told everyone that Jay was having a mid-life crisis, in her heart, she knew that Jay had fallen in love with his soulmate—something Vu had never been. For the first time, I felt Vu's humanity and vulnerability. It gave me hope that maybe we could get to the source of her self-imposed limitations. I doubled my efforts to get to the bottom of her body issues.

One day, out of the blue, I received a phone call from Vu. She was sitting in her car, at a rest stop off the freeway, crying uncontrollably. Between sobs, she said she had just dropped the children off at Jay's house, and walking down the front steps of his house, had caught a glimpse of the five of them: Jay, Diana, and the three children, laughing and teasing each other. Being a family. More specifically, being a family she wished she were a part of. Vu asked if I could meet her right away because she thought she was having a nervous breakdown. "I don't know if I'm really the best one to be calling," I told her. "What about your parents or other family members?" "No," she practically screamed, "They're the last ones I'd call. Please, Laure."

Of course, I rushed to meet Vu, and as we sat in her car, a waterfall of sadness flowed out of her. I learned that Vu's parents were first-generation immigrants from Southeast Asia who had come to America in the 1970s. The clash of old-world and modern American ways had created a difficult and traumatic childhood. Growing up, her house was a transitional home for other Southeast Asian immigrants who were trying to get their feet on the ground in a new country. While her parents had generously devoted themselves to helping others re-establish their lives, they had paid little attention to shaping the lives of their daughter and her four siblings.

Vu had grown up deprived of love and encouragement from the people that counted most: her parents. Rarely complimented for her virtues of character, the one thing people seemed to appreciate was her looks. "What a beautiful daughter you have," the visitors would tell her parents. It always seemed to please her mother and father. From this observation grew her belief that the way to earn love was to keep herself as attractive as possible. She had few other models of how to receive—or give—love. Was it any surprise she had floundered when called upon to provide nurturing, unconditional love to her husband and children?

I convinced Vu that it was vital to seek the help of a professional therapist. I also asked her to begin practicing Step Nine. When I had mentioned it before, she had always thought it seemed silly to write herself a love letter, and actually mail it. But I argued that if she wanted my help, she needed to work on the mess beneath her polished veneer.

At our next session, Vu was still recovering from her mini-breakdown, but she had been to see a therapist, which had been a tremendous relief. Convinced no American counselor would be able to understand the cultural nuances of her background, she had always dismissed therapy. But through a friend, she had found a counselor who was also Southeast Asian. He not only understood her issues, he was confident that with his help and mine, she could overcome them.

I asked about her love letter. She had used her conversation with her therapist as the starting point. She hadn't mailed the letter yet, and asked if I would read it to make sure it was "right." I laughed and told her that if I had to tell her whether or not it was "correct," she had missed the whole point. She realized her folly, but asked me to read the letter anyway.

The letter read:

Dear Vu,

I want to compliment you on your conversation with Dr. Nguyen. First of all, you went to the appointment even though it was very hard to do. You told your story honestly and courageously. You didn't leave out the bad parts. You let yourself cry. You answered his questions and didn't lie or try to make it sound better than it was. You treated it seriously. You did a good job.

Love,

Your secret admirer

I loved Vu's letter and told her so. "But that's the last time I'll read your love letters," I said. "From here on out, they're for your eyes only."

Over the next few months, a remarkable change took place in Vu. For the first time, she started believing not only that she could love herself, but that she must learn to love herself in order to fill the void that was destroying her life. She began to understand and regret the many mistakes she'd made with her family, at the same time vowing to not leave her children with the same legacy of deprivation she'd experienced as a child. While there was much time and hurt to make up for, Vu threw herself into reclaiming the love of her children. It wasn't long before she joyfully reported that the children were responding wonderfully to her efforts. Even Jay had commented on the "new Vu" and how much happier she seemed.

While I never again read Vu's letters, she told me they became a cornerstone of her recovery, helping to remind her of her own power and ability to shower herself with love.

Because one of Vu's key issues was equating physical beauty with love, I felt she needed to reinforce the worth of other qualities. Therefore, she initially focused her letters on internal characteristics: courage, honesty, kindness, etc. Eventually, she was able to also include compliments about her physical appearance without allowing them to feel more important than the internal compliments. Often with this step, I encourage clients to occasionally write their love letters in the nude. But for Vu, I did not feel this exercise was appropriate. It wasn't that she didn't need to celebrate her body—she needed to learn to celebrate what was inside.

In retrospect, Vu admitted her internal anguish had made her unlovable before her divorce. She now realized, after embracing Step Nine, that she was her greatest companion and friend.

Today, Vu remains single—happily. She hopes that, one day, she will have the opportunity to love a man as much as she has learned to love herself. But if that doesn't happen, she knows where to turn for the love and acceptance she needs: within herself. Her girls have weathered the divorce well; her son continues to need extra emotional support and attention—nurturing that Vu gives freely and lovingly.

Now when Vu talks about her relationships with her friends and children, I notice the distinct absence of negativity. When I first met Vu, she was the quintessential victim, always telling me what others had "done" to her. Now, there is a calm, soft acceptance in her demeanor that speaks volumes about how she feels about herself.

Recently when I watched Vu walk into a room, I felt her self-confidence radiating outward. She looked comfortable in her skin—which not only looks great, but attracts others to her. Now when I look at her, I see a genuinely beautiful woman. She is one of the finest examples I know of someone who made the invaluable leap from body hatred to body love.

Summary:

Step Nine is about learning to recognize and value the things we like about ourselves. We accept the opinions and standards of others too quickly, which undermines our self-esteem and personal power. To be truly happy, we must be able to tap into our own sources of self-love, without depending on the affirmations of others to feel good. Taking the time to sit down and write yourself a love letter focuses your attention on your attributes—not your failures.

Remember, writing things down makes them more believable. Stop comparing yourself to unrealistic media images. Instead, write down your special qualities in a love letter, and let that be your positive reinforcement.

Vu's willingness to examine the source of her unhappiness and her inability to love herself or others made a dramatic difference in the direction of her life.

Write your first letter based on a specific conversation where you can identify things you did well. Concentrate on character qualities, then branch out into physical attributes. If you wish, try writing your letter naked to better appreciate your body's unique virtues. Mail the letter, then open it in private. Turn this ritual into a monthly habit of renewal and redemption, and watch your self-confidence grow.

STEP 10

STAND UP STRAIGHT AND TALL.

Hostess with the Mostest

Recently, my client Kathy attended a black-tie function, without a date, at The Plaza Hotel in New York City. When we met on the day of the event, she was a nervous wreck. Kathy is a nurse in her mid-forties who is recently single. Kathy's first marriage ended fifteen years ago. She has spent the last ten years living with Sam, who is her boss Marty's best friend. The week before the gala, she and Sam broke up and he moved out. As devastated as Kathy felt, she knew she needed to pull herself together for this event, since she had been asked months before to make a speech about Marty. The event was going to include most of the staff and doctors from the hospital where she worked, with their dates. All Kathy could focus on was how freaked out she was to be dateless. She feared she would be the only one without a date, and since many of the people knew Sam, she dreaded having to repeatedly explain the situation. I attempted to talk her down from her anxiety, suggesting that she try a helpful self-esteem-building trick I've learned.

I told Kathy to go back to her apartment and pretend she was the hostess of a large and smashingly successful cocktail party—taking the lead, tending to people's needs, moving graciously around the room—being in charge of everyone having a great time. I suggested that she then carry this demeanor into the party at The Plaza. I told Kathy that I would be on-call all night if she needed to sneak off to a phone booth to call me. I didn't hear from her until the next morning.

"It was a total success—I'm never going to another party with a date again," Kathy joked, but I could tell her excitement was real. She had worn her favorite black dress, and taken extra time to get ready. When she walked into the ballroom, the first co-worker she had seen asked her where Sam was. Kathy took a deep breath, said "Beats me," grabbed a glass of champagne, and began moving around the room. Noticing that she was indeed the only "dateless wonder," Kathy was tempted to run and call me. Instead, she took a moment to breathe deeply and consciously (Step Seven), pulled herself up straight and tall, and moved into "hostess" mode. She visualized herself with perfect posture and a contagious air of self-confidence. She told herself that this was her room, her party, and everyone was taking their cue from her.

Playing hostess, she graciously struck up conversations with people from work whom she had never socialized with before. Midway through the evening, Kathy began to notice something unusual. People were gravitating toward her—as if she indeed were the hostess. More than just the attention, Kathy found herself enjoying the conversations. When it was time to deliver her speech, she had consumed enough champagne to take the edge off her nervousness. She was even feeling a little cocky. The crowd responded to her jokes, and Marty seemed genuinely touched by her sincerity. Later, she realized she had no sense of the many hours passing, since she had been focusing her attention on her speech, and the enjoyment of socializing with her cohorts.

Kathy could not believe it was 2 A.M. when she finally hailed a taxi cab. On the way home she kept re-living the evening, amazed she had had such fun without a date. When she arrived at her apartment building, the cab driver must have felt her energy, because he got out of his seat to open her door. She thanked the driver, and commented on the lively salsa music playing on his stereo. He then reached into the car, turned up the volume on the radio, took her hand, and began dancing with her in the dim morning lights of Manhattan.

Kathy said she fell asleep with a huge smile plastered across her face, feeling utterly confident and empowered.

It's amazing what this trick of "playing hostess" can do for how you carry yourself. I think it has something to do with the nurturer in all of us. When it's just ourselves we're responsible for, we can start feeling very small and unimportant. But when we're responsible for whether or not others have a good time, we suddenly pull ourselves up by our bootstraps and rise to the occasion. In turn, our attentiveness to others is flattering, and always seems to elicit a positive response.

I mean it when I say "pull ourselves up by our bootstraps." How many great hostesses do you know who slouch through their own party, slinking from guest to guest with rounded shoulders and bad posture? Not many, I'll wager. There's something about being the focal point of an occasion that makes us pull back our shoulders, pull in our stomach, and assume a wonderfully regal attitude—both mentally and physically. The question is, why wait for rare occasions to showcase our best presentation of ourselves? The fact is, we are the hostess of a very special occasion, every day: our own lives.

Grandmother Was Right

I can spot a dancer walking down the street from a mile away. The reason is her tall postural confidence, and her assured steps. There is nothing more impressive than the sight of someone who carries herself with a lifted, erect posture.

Dancer or not, there is no reason you can't imitate this body confidence. It is a simple secret that can shave ten or more pounds from your midsection— instantly. If you practice what good posture looks like, you will begin to feel the internal power of confidence. The image you project will be a vision of self-empowerment and health.

My grandmother used to admonish, "Stand up straight, and pull your stomach in." I used to feel so irritated at her constant nagging. In retrospect, I now understand and appreciate her advice. In accepting myself as I am today (Step Nine), I always remain extremely conscious of my body placement and posture. I learned this lesson years ago, when I suffered through a miserable hip injury. The injury taught me the importance and necessity of carrying my body correctly. As I have grown older, this postural awareness has become increasingly valuable, ensuring a pain-free, confident stance.

Standing up straight and tall is like giving yourself an internal tune-up. On the other hand, poor posture puts unnecessary stress on your entire body, making you appear many pounds heavier. In *Precision Training for Body and Mind,* Karen Voight recommends testing your posture by having someone measure the distance between your shoulder blades when you're in a typical stance. If they are six to eight inches apart, your upper body is probably rounded, portraying a hunched posture. If this space is only four to six inches apart, your posture is probably erect with upper body balance.

Learning what happens to your body as you age, while understanding the impact of posture, can help determine how you will look—and feel—as you get older. In our early forties, height reduction begins. Although this initial change is unnoticeable, it is the result of a weakened skeletal structure in the spine. The average woman shrinks two inches by the end of her seventies. This skeletal deterioration, and the internal complications it causes, is amplified by poor posture and minimized by good posture. It is no secret that improving your posture helps the biomechanics of your body, aiding its ability to move and function properly. As well, correct postural alignment helps breathing and respiratory functions, while preventing back pain, fatigue, and other aches and problems.

I begin my postural awareness the moment I wake up in the morning. Before popping up out of bed, I take the time to stretch my body. Never go directly from a supine position (lying down) to a sitting position. Instead, take a few extra moments to thoughtfully awaken. While lying in bed, stretch both arms over your head, taking several deep breaths, and pulling in your abdominal muscles. As you push your spine toward the mattress, feel the length of your body. Take a few moments to visualize your goals for the day. Focus on a positive impression of yourself. Then roll over to a fetal position, slowly pushing your body weight through your arms and hands to lift up to a sitting position. Sit up tall, tuck in your abdominal muscles, lift your head high, take a few deep breaths, and then leave your bed to begin your day with mental and physical awareness.

Tape up message reminders around your house to "stand up straight," "walk tall," "walk like a dancer," "pull in your stomach," etc. If you have a job that requires many hours of sitting, take breaks throughout the day. Get up, walk around, drink water (Step Two), take a stretch. Visualize yourself one inch taller. Carry yourself as if you are being pulled up by a cord attached to the top of your head. When you feel your physical essence, carrying your body with a lifted posture and a pleasant smile, it translates into empowerment. Try it while you are sitting at your desk, or standing in line, or walking through the grocery aisles. You will find that the response you get is incredibly fulfilling.

The Fine Art of Stripping

Good posture is mostly about contracting your abdominal muscles, breathing consciously, and holding your head high while pressing your shoulders down. Enhancing your mental certainty is as valuable as perfecting your body placement. One of the greatest ways to develop mental self-confidence is to privately strip for yourself.

I am convinced that naked anxiety is a gender issue. When the subject of nakedness comes up with clients, I often think about Tyler, my six-year-old stepson. Saying the word "naked" is enough to send him into hysterical laughter. One day, when he was three, I decided to test him by saying, "naked bananas," "naked flowers," "naked dinosaurs." Each time I said the word "naked," he would giggle uncontrollably. Likewise, the men I train think naked anything sounds like fun. However, women, generally appear undeniably anxious at the mere mention of the word. Women are so obsessed with comparing themselves to other women assuming they "should" look a certain way to be physically acceptable. This female habit inevitably sabotages any opportunity to be happy in our bodies. How sad and unnecessary!

Physical fear is based on the messages we receive from our minds. Our bodies emulate what our minds communicate, thus we typically exude discomfort. My hopeful belief is that once you understand your uncomfortable feelings, you can choose how to react when receiving these fearful messages. As I mentioned in Step Three, when we make the mind-body connection, it's as if we suddenly realize our bodies have been screaming at us for years, we just had the volume turned down, for fear of what we might hear.

As I have mentioned many times in this book, the ultimate definition of self-confidence is being comfortable with yourself naked. If you are comfortable being nude, you can take yourself anywhere in the world—dressed, with or without a companion. We can teach ourselves this power, although sometimes we have to relearn it, as you will see in the upcoming story. Once you can visualize what self-confidence looks like (Step Six), you can achieve it.

How can you learn to be comfortable with your naked body? In addition to my ten steps, stripping can be a powerful route toward self-confidence. How can you hope to achieve the liberation that comes with stripping for no one but yourself? Desire is a crucial part of the process. It's not an easy journey; however, it will inevitably be worth the challenges. Our bodies are like multilayered friends, dependable and reliable. As with a good friend, once we desire to know our bodies and minds, the possibilities are miraculous and endless.

I hope my story will help you find the motivation to start the journey.

My Story

I want to begin my story by relating a recent event involving this book which was very humbling and revealing. When my editor and I decided that I would pose naked for the cover, at first I felt excited. Within days, however, excitement turned into anxiety, and anxiety quickly evolved into fear. As my stomach churned, and insomnia set in, I knew I needed some private time (Step Eight) to understand what was going on.

Initially I thought it was fear of who the photographer might be. It's hard enough to bond with a photographer when dressed. The last thing I wanted was to find myself uncomfortable with someone—and naked. I reminded myself to practice what I preach—that it was about how I felt about myself. If I felt good naked, that's all that should matter; my comfort would be evident in the picture. I was even able to laugh at the irony of my predicament. Yet the fear lingered. Deep down, I knew that my anxiety was not just about the photographer. I traveled to the next layer of fear. What came up as the source of my stress may surprise you.

I am heavier than I have been in my adult life. I am what romance novelists would call "full-fleshed and lusty." While I don't weigh myself, I would guess that I am twenty pounds heavier than five years ago, when I was leading eight- to ten aerobics classes a day. Of course, that buff body, while an achievement by Hollywood standards, reflected a life that was far less balanced than my life is now. Today, I am happier, more relaxed, and much more tuned in to my mind-body connection. Embracing my "robust" body in the course of normal everyday life is one thing. Plastering it on the cover of a book is quite another. I continued to fret. At my most exposed, I had to admit that I feared all of my old hard-body friends thinking I looked . . . well, fat. I could just hear people saying:

"Did you see Laure's book?"
"Yeah, can you believe how heavy she is?"
"I can't believe she would ever let anyone photograph her naked, looking like that."
"That takes guts."

We all know that true friends would never say anything like that. But fear-induced mind-sets die hard, even when you combat them daily for a living.

I decided to call Juana, my best female friend, and ask her what she thought. She said I should absolutely pose naked for the cover; that my body is a reflection of my program and it shows that I'm willing to practice what I preach. She also suggested that I call our photographer friend, Jerry Schatzberg, and talk to him.

Juana had introduced me to Jerry Schatzberg years earlier while I was going through my divorce. Jerry is a talented photographer and filmmaker who, at the time, was working on a project that showcased female nudes. His images did not include faces, just bodies. Juana had posed for him and expressed how liberating it was. She explained that his focus was on finding the unique beauty in every woman, no matter what her shape or size. She suggested that I sit for him. I told her I was more comfortable first meeting him and seeing his pictures.

I was instantly comfortable with Jerry. Juana's pictures were fantastic. Seeing her naked body, without her face, completely changed the experience of looking at her body parts. They looked like pieces of fruit, or fabulous landscapes. He had photographed a number of women in addition to Juana. Their bodies could not have been more different. One had really wild scars. One was quite overweight. Yet through the vision of his lens, they all looked truly beautiful. Jerry and I talked about our shared mission to help women feel good about their bodies. I knew I wanted to be his next subject.

My body, at that time, was a work of art, in some ways more masculine than feminine with all of its tone and definition. My divorce had motivated the hell out of me. I was sad and lonely, and found working out to be healing therapy. I was also training clients, as well as choreographing my new video series. Yet even with a buff body, and an understanding photographer who went out of his way to make me feel comfortable, I was terrified the first hour of the shoot.

Then Jerry said something that caught me completely off guard. He asked me to stand up straighter. I did a double take. Me—the posture-perfect girl—slouching? He saw my raised eyebrows and shared that one way women exhibit their fear of being naked is to try and minimize their bodies by collapsing their shoulders and rounding their spines. I suddenly flashed on all those naked bodies in the locker room of my studio—all slouched over and scurrying to quickly cover themselves. It's a myth, of course, that hunching over does anything to mitigate the impact of a naked body. I realized that if I was going to pose nude, I might as well stand up tall and quit acting like I was in freshman P.E. class.

It's amazing what this simple body adjustment did for my attitude and perspective. By the second hour, it felt completely natural, actually fun to be naked. When my photo session ended, I told Jerry about the mental roller coaster I had experienced during the session, and the power of adjusting my posture. He listened knowingly, and acknowledged my courage. I left his apartment feeling like I had bungee-jumped off the Chrysler building.

What a kick it was to see my pictures. Was that really my body? The forms were so beautiful, artistic, long and languid. I felt very proud of myself. Jerry shared stories about the other women he had photographed, discussing the fear and aversion that all women experience at the notion of being naked. I was awestruck by the power of being comfortable naked, and the way good-old-fashioned posture helped me cast away fear and embrace the full beauty of my body.

Unfortunately, in my crisis over posing for this book, I was having serious trouble remembering the simple wisdom I had gleaned from that first photo session. I called Jerry, as Juana suggested, and talked about my book. A conflict of schedules made it impossible for him to do the photo shoot. But he agreed that my naked image was the perfect concept for the cover.

I told him, "You don't know what I look like now. My body is not the same body you photographed before."
"What do you mean?"
"Well, I'm much more womanly . . . in fact, twenty pounds more womanly."
"Laure, do you remember what you said to me when I photographed you then?"
"What?"
"You warned me that you had a boy's body and that it wasn't very feminine."
I laughed and said, "Well, now it's pure femininity."
He replied, "Good, because your voice sounds happy, and you seem much calmer. Stand up straight and you'll be beautiful."

Talking to Jerry brought back other memories. I realized that my old body wasn't necessarily a comfortable body to live in. I remembered how aggressive and tense I had felt in my perfectly taut shape. In retrospect, my body, twenty pounds ago, felt separate from my female soul. It did not feel nurtured or nourished. Impressive, yes, but not fully integrated with my female spirituality.

We hung up and I thought about his comments.

Of course, he was right. I am more content in my life today, and my body is a reflection of that peace and serenity. My life now includes a wonderful marriage, a satisfying career, and the fulfillment of parenting two incredible children. I no longer crave three hours at the gym each day. Instead I prefer scheduling walking and light jogging (Step Four) over sprints. I choose stretching, yoga, meditation, and breathing (Step Seven) over pumping iron and straining to lift heavy weights. Sometimes I only have ten minutes to exercise (Step Three), and that's okay. Most important, when I don't focus on what others will think of the way I look, which is a huge waste of time and energy anyway, I feel great naked. And I do feel more sensual and feminine with the extra pounds I now carry.

I decided what I needed to do to embrace my fuller body, and prepare for the cover photo session, was to strip for myself. I waited until I was alone in the house. I turned out the lights and lit all of my candles. I blasted my favorite Annie Lennox tunes and began a slow, sultry dance around the room. I stood up tall, straight, and proud, listening as my spine popped happily into alignment. As I tore off my tank top and my oversized men's boxer shorts, I giggled at the fun and freedom of being totally alive inside. I recognized this feeling—it was the same one I'd had leaving Jerry's studio years before; the same feeling I have whenever I can revel in the sheer wonder of my own naked self. Don't underestimate the power of naked physical freedom—whether you're a three-year-old running around the house after a bath, or a forty-three-year-old running around your bedroom. It is an essential aspect of confronting and embracing yourself.

I emerged from my brief lapse into old thought patterns ready to show off my lusty, luscious, full-fleshed self. I found a woman photographer named Sharon Amestoy who seemed to share Jerry's appreciation of the female form. She also related to the mission of my book.

The photo session was a wonderful experience. I strode onto the set, head high, shoulders back, chin up, acting like the hostess of my own very exclusive soiree. I could have been carrying forty extra pounds and not cared. Since the support crew was all female, the best parts of the day were the conversations that ensued about the female body. I hope you can see in the final cover photograph how confident and comfortable I felt that day.

What I keep coming back to is how women are so much more alike than different. We all think about the same issues regarding our bodies. We all fret and worry about the way our thighs look, our stomachs bulge, our bosoms differ, our buttocks spread, our fleshy arms, our thick backs, our full faces. And at the end of this vicious destructive cycle, we hopefully learn, before we die, that our true value as human beings has nothing to do with how much we weigh or what size clothes we wear.

What matters is our health, our strength, our integrity, our opinion, our sense of self-worth, our love for others, our contributions to the world we live in, and our acceptance of ourselves as individuals. Our ability to walk tall and proud into any room, any time, with or without an escort, while remaining authentic to ourselves.

My sincere hope is that this book has helped you begin your process toward self-knowledge and empowerment. I have faith that my ten steps will assist you in developing harmony between your body, mind, and soul. I also believe that by learning more about yourself, you can find happiness and joy you may not have thought possible. I know it can happen, because I experienced such a transformation myself. And I've marveled as I have witnessed it in scores of women like you.

Until every woman can eat chocolate naked, stand in front of a mirror naked, repeat affirmations naked, examine her best features naked, dance naked, stand up straight and tall naked, and otherwise rejoice in her unique and miraculous body, it will be up to each of us to help put an end to female body hatred.

Because every woman deserves to feel good naked.

Summary:

Step Ten is about an old secret that is more powerful than you can imagine. If you practice what self-confidence looks like, you will begin to experience what it feels like. If you need a mental trick for motivation, play-act the role of a charming hostess.

My grandmother always told me to stand up straight, pull in my stomach, and smile. She was right. Try it while you're sitting at your desk, or standing in line at the grocery. The response you will get is incredibly fulfilling.

There is no question that mind-body confidence is the ultimate beauty secret. By improving your body placement and self-assurance, you will also improve your overall health. Better still, good posture will shave ten pounds off your appearance immediately.

After practicing what self-confidence looks like on the outside to others, try a private striptease to nurture what self-confidence feels like on the inside.

Finally, just as I did when old mind-sets came creeping back into my psyche, rely on people you love and trust to remind you what's important in a balanced, joy-filled, feel-good-naked life. Embrace those qualities with gusto!

ARE YOU IN BALANCE?

While no one is able to achieve a life that is perfect in every regard, I firmly believe we can all aspire to a balanced life. The question is, what constitutes "balanced"? The following quiz is a measure I developed to help women assess the degree of balance and sanity in their lives. Answer each question honestly, and when more than one response seems to fit, choose the answer which is most typical for you.

A Quiz

1. When your clothes start feeling tight, what are you most likely to do?
a) Carry yourself with a more confident body posture
b) Figure out ways to exercise more
c) Alter your food intake
d) Buy new clothes

2. To lose weight by monitoring your food intake, what are you most likely to do?
a) Eat five small but well-balanced mini-meals
b) Cut a specific food group (i.e., sweets, carbohydrates) from your diet
c) Follow the latest fad diet
d) Skip meals

3. If you experience a late-afternoon drop in your energy, what are you most likely to do?
a) Take a brisk walk
b) Lie down for a quick nap
c) Go for a tall double espresso or soda
d) Head to the vending machine for a snack

4. If you must work overtime, what are you most likely to give up?
a) Watching your favorite TV program
b) Social plans
c) A meal
d) Exercise

5. If you find yourself with fifteen extra minutes, what are you most likely to do?
a) Read, meditate, or enjoy being still and quiet
b) Take a walk
c) Talk on the phone or watch TV
d) Snack

6. Do you fantasize about having the body of a super model or celebrity?
a) Hardly ever
b) Sometimes
c) Often
d) All the time

7. In a high-stress situation, what are you most likely to do?
a) Concentrate on breathing deeply while staying calm
b) Take charge
c) Take out your stress on others by being short or snippy
d) Eat

8. Which best describes how you feel when you are alone?
a) Relaxed
b) Not great, but able to tolerate it
c) Eager to find someone to call or get together with
d) Fearful and distraught

9. When you feel sad, what are you most likely to do?
a) Cry freely as needed
b) Not cry, but allow your feelings to creep out in other ways
c) Bury your feelings
d) Become depressed for long periods of time

10. If you feel unhappy in a relationship, what are you most likely to do?
a) Share your feelings with your partner and prepare to work on possible solutions
b) Leave the relationship
c) Blame yourself
d) Continue on as if nothing is wrong

11. **In difficult interactions with others, what are you most likely to do?**
a) Stay emotionally clear-headed
b) Back down and avoid confrontation
c) Get defensive and overly emotional, determined to prove yourself right
d) Be emotionally devastated, both during the incident and for a long time afterward

12. **When eating "treats," what do you do?**
a) Not care who is around while eating them
b) Prefer sharing with others
c) Prefer eating treats by yourself so you can eat more
d) Always eat by yourself, often bingeing

13. **Which most closely describes your relationship with alcohol?**
a) Can take it or leave it
b) Enjoy one or two glasses of wine with dinner and/or lunch
c) Drink sporadically but am sometimes impacted the next day
d) Drink frequently and am often impacted the next day

14. **If your feelings are hurt, what are you most likely to do?**
a) Face the feelings, while considering your mood and whether or not the slight was intentional
b) Talk to the person about your feelings
c) Say something hurtful back
d) Do a slow burn in silence, vowing revenge

15. **In general, are you most likely to say:**
a) "I'd like to, but I don't think I can commit right now."
b) "Maybe. Let me check my schedule and get back to you."
c) "Um . . . I really shouldn't . . . but . . . okay, I guess so."
d) "Sure, I'll take care of that." (Repeated numerous times daily)

Give yourself one point for each "a" answer, three points for each "b" answer, five points for each "c" answer and seven points for each "d" answer. Add up your totals. Here's what the numbers may tell you about whether or not your life is in balance.

15–37: You understand the importance of moderation and healthy self-care. You may have a few indulgent vices and problem points, but they aren't jeopardizing your ability to be good to yourself. You probably feel good naked!

38–60: You are in dangerous territory. You are probably getting by for the most part, but every now and then, things go haywire in your life and you're not sure why—or how to get on a saner track. You are at risk of falling into more unhealthy habits and becoming truly unhappy with your personal image and your body. You only feel good naked—sometimes.

61–83: You feel out of control in several key areas of your life. A gnawing sense of dissatisfaction and repeated commitments to do something about problematic issues has not been enough to motivate you to take action—so far. You don't feel good naked.

84–105: You are very unhappy about the direction of your life choices. You feel like a spectator watching your life whirl by, unable to take steps to change the desperate, overwhelming feelings that keep growing inside. You doubt that you have the character or courage to make a personal plan to improve. You don't feel good about yourself dressed, let alone naked.

Whatever you scored, continue to incorporate the ten *Feel Good Naked* steps into your life. Remember, these steps are designed to help you achieve more balance in your daily life without requiring huge, unrealistic adjustments in your schedule.

Take this quiz every month and compare your scores. As your score gets lower, feel proud that you have taken conscious steps toward a less stressful, more balanced life.

THE TOP 10 FEMALE BODY QUESTIONS

1. Is it possible to get rid of cellulite?

According to the American Dietetic Association's Complete Food & Nutrition Guide, "cellulite is simply normal body fat under the skin that looks lumpy when the fat layer gets thick, allowing connective, fibrous-looking tissue that holds fat in place to show." In other words, cellulite is just a fancy word for fat. Because the structure of fat cells differs between genders, women are more prone to these lumpy fat deposits than men. What's more, some women are more susceptible to cellulite than other women, due to factors such as age and genetics.

What can you do about it? The best remedy is exercise, which increases the amount of fat your body burns and therefore reduces fat deposits. Exercise is also a wonderful way to firm muscles, smoothing the appearance of cellulite-prone areas (see Step Three). Take a daily walk and learn how to properly perform forward and backward lunges. Sign up for a toning class at your local gym. Activate your body whenever you have the opportunity, i.e., take stairs instead of escalators or elevators, park in the far end of the parking lot, walk instead of driving, play with your children, etc. Also, drink plenty of water each day. This helps the skin from the inside out (Step Two).

It's also a good idea to look at your fat intake, although without exercise, cutting back on fatty foods alone won't necessarily rid your body of cellulite. Read the Nutritional Facts that accompany all foods. Try sticking with my favorite formula—no more than three grams of fat per 100 calories. Notice the amount of high-fat foods you currently eat. Make up your mind to choose low- or no-fat versions if they are available.

For example:
- skim milk or one percent milk instead of whole milk
- low-fat or baked snacks instead of fried snacks
- nonfat yogurt instead of regular yogurt
- low-fat salad dressings, sauces, and condiments
- sorbet instead of ice cream
- fat-free cottage or cream cheese instead of regular cheese
- non-fat yogurt instead of sour cream

Take a look at your grandmother, mother, and other female relatives to see what your genetic predisposition to cellulite looks like.

By the way, forget body creams or potions that claim to rid your body of cellulite! While a number of recent studies have investigated the effectiveness of "thigh creams" in ridding the body of cellulite, none have shown any significant degree of success.

2. How can I get myself to stick with the commitments I make to improve my body?

Make them as easy to incorporate into your life as possible. If you know that changing clothes and driving to a gym will become a drag, make your exercise choices something simple you can do in any clothes, inside your home. If you know you'll forget to drink water, buy a plastic sport bottle and keep it always with you. If thirty minutes of private time seven days a week seems too daunting, make it only five days a week and leave your weekends open (Steps Two, Three, and Eight).

3. If I commit to an exercise routine, when can I expect to see results?

Ever heard the phrase "individual results may vary"? There's a reason for it, namely that everyone's body responds differently to increased physical activity. Key variables are the body's condition when you start the program and the intricacies of your body's metabolism. It is vital to understand that you might not see real results on your body for three to six weeks. This is the hard part—you must find a way to stay motivated until you see visual changes. Once the payback starts—in the form of muscle definition, increased stamina, and weight loss—it becomes your incentive to stick with your program. Trust me, these changes will happen, and they'll be a powerful motivator! Until then, here's my three-point survival plan:

a. Write down your workout schedule each Sunday for the upcoming week. If it's on paper, you'll take it more seriously (Step Four).
b. Schedule workouts with a neighbor, friend, or co-worker, to ensure that someone is depending on you to show up. You'll be less likely to cancel your sessions.
c. Cut out a photo of someone whose body or posture you admire, and whose body type is similar to yours. Tape it to your bathroom mirror (Step Six).

4. Is it realistic to think that I can really change my body?

You cannot change your body type or frame, i.e., small upper body/big hips, big breasts/big hips, large back/no hips, etc. However, you can certainly change your body within the parameters of its basic frame. We all have the potential to have healthy bodies. The key for real change is to effectively incorporate the components of fitness into your daily life:

a. cardiovascular activity
b. resistance training
c. stretching/flexibility

Remember, everyone's body changes at a different pace. Some are faster than others. It can be quite frustrating when no visible changes are recognized. However, remain consistent with your routine and changes will eventually occur. Don't give up! Real changes take real time.

5. Is it advisable to purchase fitness equipment for my home?

Yes, but make sure to purchase high-quality equipment so that your investment stands the test of time—kids, husbands, etc. I also recommend that if you're going to purchase equipment, make it an aerobic, total-body choice such as a motorized treadmill with incline features, cross-country ski machine, rowing machine, stair climber with handles for upper body work, etc., as opposed to a gimmicky spot-reducer.

Home fitness equipment can help you overcome motivation-busters such as bad weather, scheduling problems, and the hassles of driving to and from the gym. With home fitness equipment, you can utilize a sudden windfall of free time (Steps Three and Eight). It's there waiting for you, twenty-four hours a day, rain or shine.

6. In trying to juggle the demands of marriage, career, and children, how can I possibly find time for myself?

Women's stress levels have never been higher. It is impossible to manage a relationship, a career, and parenting responsibilities equally well at all times. Give yourself a mental break as often as possible. Delegate tasks to others. Ask neighbors and friends for favors. Realize that if you take a personal day from work, it will all still be there tomorrow.

Insist on taking quiet, alone time for yourself each and every day (Steps Seven and Eight). If you can't find thirty minutes, find twenty, or ten or even five. The act of taking even the smallest break for yourself is as important as the break itself.

If you don't take care of everyone else, they'll figure it out. You deserve a break and the only one who can give it to you is you!

7. I'm doing everything right—eating better and exercising. Why can't I lose weight?

Every body has a set point weight—a weight at which your body runs most comfortably. This is a weight that your body will always naturally gravitate to. As you learned with Susan in Step Four, if your set point is at a weight that feels too heavy, it will require extra effort to lose more. That can mean adding to your exercise time, and eating not only healthier but perhaps less.

Be brutally honest about your true intake of calories. Are you counting the leftovers on your child's plate that you can't stand to see go to waste? Are you counting the appetizers you snack on before dinner? Do you know how many calories are in that delicious calzone you have twice a week for lunch at your favorite restaurant? To get past a weight plateau you have to eat consciously and with awareness (Step Five).

Consider that even though your set point weight may not be model perfect, it may be the best weight for you. As long as you're fit and healthy, ask yourself if your expectations are simply unrealistic for your body.

Remember, Marilyn Monroe was a size fourteen.

8. Will a low-carbohydrate diet help me lose weight?

In today's confusing nutritional world, this is a common question. Years ago we were told to "carbo load." Today, we are told that carbohydrates make us fat!

In their book *Fad-Free Nutrition,* health experts Dr. Frederick Stare and Elizabeth Whelan explain, "Any diet that deviates from sound nutrition principles should be viewed with suspicion . . . . They may advocate no fat or no carbohydrates . . . . All such diets are useless, and many are health hazards."

They go on to say, "You cannot achieve permanent weight control until you learn how to handle, in moderation, all of the foods that make up a nutritionally balanced diet." That means some carbohydrates, some dairy and protein, some fat, and lots of fruits and vegetables. One of my rules when grocery shopping is to always buy fresh. The fresher a food, the higher its vitamin and nutrient content, especially fruits and vegetables. Go to the grocery store and open your eyes to what is in season. If peaches are in season, buy peaches. If halibut is the freshest fish of the day, buy halibut.

Stay away from nutritionally empty foods, such as sodas, chips, crackers, and candies. These foods will make you fat while providing no nutritional value. Splurging once in a while is fine, but for sound health—and the surest way to long-lasting weight control—eat balanced meals, eat what is fresh, and eat with awareness (Steps One and Five).

9. Should I consider liposuction for my abdominal area if I can't seem to get my stomach flat?

I'm a big opponent of plastic surgery for non-obese fat reduction. Of course, if you have a serious problem that is endangering your health, and your doctor recommends surgery as the only option, that's another story. However, if it's just for the sake of vanity, forget it! As far as we've come in medical advances, surgery is still an invasion of the body, with all the attendant risks of complications, infection, etc. It's a rare case that's worth the risks, hassles, or money. Often, plastic surgery is merely a Band-Aid, masking the real problem of self-dissatisfaction. It's another shortcut attempt to find inner happiness through outer means.

One of my favorite women is a fifty-one year old named Bonnie. Bonnie is bright, bubbly, has mothered three children, and carries herself proudly and assuredly. Bonnie listens to her body; she eats what she craves, hikes on weekends, and plays actively with her children. People are always amazed when she openly tells them what she weighs, because it's so much more than what you would guess, based on the way she stands, walks, and holds her body. Recently when I ran into Bonnie, she shared with me that one of our mutual friends had just "gone under the knife," having a face and eye lift. We both agreed that this woman did not need either. Together, we pondered why she had elective surgery, agreeing that our friend's issues were more psychological than physical. As we said our good-byes, I watched Bonnie walk away with her trademark confidence, wishing I could bottle some of it for our friend.

Forget the liposuction. There are no shortcuts to loving your body—and yourself—naked.

10. What is the single simplest, most effective thing I can do to enhance my appearance?

Stand up straight! As my friend Bonnie, whom I just mentioned, and millions of other women have discovered, this is the little-known secret to instantaneously losing ten pounds. It's also a great way to strengthen and empower your abdominal and back muscles (Step Ten).

A LOVER'S PERSPECTIVE

Nothing contributes more to the success of a self-enhancement program than having the encouragement of those we love. If you are the "significant other" of someone who is reading this book and embarking on the ten-step *Feel Good Naked* program, your role as supporter and cheerleader cannot be overstated.

Especially if you are a man who doesn't "get" why your lover doesn't feel good naked, it is important for you to understand how pervasive female body hatred is. According to the ThriveOnline Web site and the National Women's Health Resource Center:

- Seven million women in the U.S. suffer from eating disorders
- Ninety-five percent of American women overestimate their body size
- Two-thirds of American women place "fear of getting fat" on their list of life's worst fears

In a survey in which two hundred women were asked, "If you could change one thing about your body, what would it be?" not one woman said she would leave her body unchanged!

Your wife or girlfriend is neither crazy nor unusual. But she does need to take action to counteract her negative body perception(s). This program helps her do that—sometimes in unconventional ways that may require understanding and patience on your part. By providing unconditional support, however, you will reap countless tangible rewards. Over time, you will notice that your partner has become happier, less frazzled, more self-assured, and both sexier and more sexual in the ways she perceives and carries herself. And what could be more desirable and appealing to you as her lover?

Don't go overboard in your support, and push too hard. This is a path that she must find for herself, in her own time. Yet with your loving reassurance and gentle affirmations, her journey will be infinitely easier and more successful. Which ultimately will help you both feel good naked!

And . . . don't be surprised to find yourself investigating the ten steps once you've witnessed the profound improvements in your lover's self-esteem.

FEEL GOOD NAKED
10-STEP SUMMARY

Make a copy of this page and tack it up on a wall so you can be reminded each day of these ten no-diet secrets:

1. DON'T DEPRIVE YOURSELF—TREAT YOURSELF ONCE A WEEK

2. DRINK WATER, DRINK WATER, DRINK WATER

3. WATCH 10 MINUTES OF EXERCISE A DAY CHANGE YOUR FACE AND YOUR LIFE

4. SCHEDULE FITNESS APPOINTMENTS IN WRITING EACH WEEK

5. DON'T STOP EATING—STOP EATING IN FRONT OF THE TV

6. PICK AN IDOL AND LET THAT PERSON MOTIVATE YOU

7. BREATHE CONSCIOUSLY FOR 5 MINUTES EVERY DAY

8. TAKE 30 MINUTES OF PRIVATE TIME EACH DAY

9. WRITE YOURSELF A LOVE LETTER ONCE A MONTH

10. STAND UP STRAIGHT AND TALL

For more information, visit my Web site at www.feelgoodnaked.com.

SERENITY PRAYER

Grant me the serenity to accept the things I cannot change;
the courage to change the things I can;
and the wisdom to know the difference.

Bibliography

Anorexia Nervosa and Bulimia Association. Eating Disorders. (Online) http://www.ams.queensu.ca/anab/moreinfo.htm.

Bauman, Alisa, Sari Harrar, and the editors of Prevention Health Books, *Fat to Firm at Any Age*. Emmaus, Pennsylvania: Rodale Press, 1998.

Campbell, Don and Al Lee, "Waiting to Inhale," *The Oregonian*, May 21, 2000.

Duyff, Roberta L., M.S., R.D., C.F.C.S. The American Dietetic Association's Complete Food and Nutrition Guide. Minneapolis: Chronimed Publishing, 1998.

"Eating with Teens Improves Their Level of Adjustment." Behavioral Health Treatment, September, 1997.

Greene, Bob and Oprah Winfrey. *Make the Connection: Ten Steps to a Better Body and a Better Life*. New York: Hyperion, 1996.

Hay, Louise. *You Can Heal Your Life*. Santa Monica: Hay House, 1984.

Henner, Marilu. *Marilu Henner's Total Health Makeover*. New York: HarperCollins Publishers, Inc., 1998.

Hornbacher, Marya. *Wasted: A Memoir of Anorexia and Bulimia*. New York: HarperCollins Publishing, 1998.

"How TV Puts on Pounds." *Environmental Nutrition*, May, 1998.

Kortge, Carolyn Scott. *The Spirited Walker: Fitness Walking for Clarity, Balance, and Spiritual Connection*. New York: HarperCollins Publishers Inc., 1998.

Laborde, Karen. "Stressing the Issue: the Mind/Body Connection." *New Orleans Magazine*, October, 1997.

Rombauer, Irma and Marion Rombauer Becker. *Joy of Cooking*. Indianapolis: Bobbs-Merrill Company, 1975.

Ronzio, Robert A., Ph.D., C.N.S., F.A.I.C. *The Encyclopedia of Nutrition and Good Health*. New York: Facts on File, 1997.

Stare, Frederick J., M.D. and Elizabeth Whelan, Sc.D., M.P.H. *Fad-Free Nutrition*. Alameda: Hunter House Inc., 1998.

Stough, Carl and Reece Stough. *Dr. Breath: The Story of Breathing Coordination*. New York: William Morrow and Company, Inc., 1970.

Strahl, Marsha. "Standing Tall." *American Fitness*. March, 1998.

ThriveOnline and the National Women's Health Resource Center. (Online) Body Image Quiz. http://www.thriveonline.com.

Voight, Karen. *Precision Training for Body and Mind.* New York: Hyperion Publishing, 1996.

Waterhouse, Debra, M.P.H., R.D. *Outsmarting the Female Fat Cell.* New York: Hyperion, 1993.

Notes

_____

_____

_____

_____

_____

_____

_____

_____

_____

_____

_____

_____

_____

_____

_____

_____

_____

_____

_____

_____

_____

_____